CP Time No More

Not A Book of Color…This Book Will Help Us All!

By

TJ Coleman

CP Time No More
Not A Book Of Color...This Book Will Help Us All!
by TJ Coleman

Printed in the United States of America

ISBN 9781619049260

Unless otherwise indicated, Bible quotations are taken from The King James Version of the Bible.

www.xulonpress.com

Only God can cause a man to feel the heart of a woman. Only God can cause a man to understand the depth of hurt the heart of a woman can bear at hands of a man. TJ was given such a cause. Chosen and instructed by God, TJ expresses an unusual understanding of a woman's heart and hurt caused by man. In his writing, he conveys clearly and fully man's need for self-accountability, and communicates it in the form of a well articulated apology.

Men; since this book is written by a man, you will hear a man's voice and it will let you know you are not alone. Moreover, you will hear the voice of all men who are, like you, ready to receive God-given correction and the acceptance of God-given responsibility. In this correction and acceptance, you will find and fulfill the role and purpose for which you were created. Do not be quick to reject the words in this book. For in doing so, you may also, in turn, reject your purpose.

Women; prepare to forgive. Prepare for healing. Prepare to have the protective wall you have built around your heart, brick by pain filled brick, to be torn down. And, prepare to build walls no more.

Robin Benjamin

TABLE OF CONTENTS

INTRODUCTION

Assignments from God are not Optional!

WORDS FROM THE SCRIBE

I have very little to do with the writings in this book although I typed every one of them. Although ever word, sentence and paragraph came through my mind, I can't take any credit for not even one word.

Over 20 years ago, God sent a word of prophecy into my life. His words were, "I will speak to you like Moses!" I didn't have a clue what that meant, but I would find out. I learned that everyone God used in the Bible to do great things, they all had one thing in common...They suffered!

They suffered for God's benefit and their own. I would walk a similar road of suffering. At the age of 40, healthy and reaching my goals in my career, I was disabled from my job. The job that I took to advance my career ended up ruining it. Within two years of working my new job, I became 80% disabled. By the third year, I was 100% disabled.

I was placed off work for 30 days at a time by my physician. I would sneak into work when I was supposed to be off. I was finally told I wouldn't get any better by my physician if I didn't stop working. I listened.

I was placed off work for 5 months, expecting to return the entire time. I had every procedure to assist me with the debilitating pain I was in, but nothing worked. Finally, my doctor gave me the news. "Mr. Coleman, I know you want to go back to work, but you have some very serious injuries and you'll never be able to work again!"

I was devastated! Not only was I in tremendous pain, now my career was over! Depressed, I thought God had forgotten all about me and all the words He's spoken over my life. Now my life was filled with excruciating pain in four or more places in my body every day. This was not the path I'd chosen for my life. Yet, there was no escaping the pain.

A shell of my former self, I moved back home to West Virginia, as I couldn't even physically take care of myself. My memory suffered due to being depressed and I couldn't even drive anymore. I moved home to be closer to my family for help. It was humbling, but when you hurt as bad as I did, you have no shame. It was like back in the day when I used to drink. I would never dare put my face near a toilet seat, but when you're throwing up drunk, all shame leaves you and the toilet becomes your best friend!

For the first three years of my return home, I slept most of the time just to escape the pain in my body. I wondered; where was God in all this? My faith hung on by a thread.

Suddenly, something happened to me. I would hear a voice speaking words to me. It was a soft, gentle voice. The words I heard were full of wisdom and revelation knowledge. The intelligence was far greater than mine. Quickly, I recognized this was the voice of God, as He reminded me of the word He spoke into my life over 20 years ago, "I will speak to you like Moses!"

Suddenly, I understood and quickly learned to be obedient to what I heard and learned to write down the words He spoke to me. Soon, I was carrying my iPod with me everywhere I went, as these words came to me constantly and without notice. I learned to be available for God whenever he wanted to speak to me.

I was His servant now! I now understood this was my purpose and everything that previously happened to me in my life, led me to this place. No, I wasn't a writer, but I would become a scribe for The Master. I would write as He spoke to me. Within two months I had an entire book 12 chapters long.

Within the two years since God has given me this gift, I've completed seven books and I'm well into the eighth one. I start a new book at 200 pages. Each page is different. Each writing is different. God picks the subjects, the words and the times He speaks to me. I've learned to just be obedient to His voice.

I would quickly learn that these words weren't for me, but for Humanity! It's a special privilege of hearing God speak to us in our own language, in our own times, in the situations that we live and find ourselves today. His words were clear, easily understood and not in parables and mysteries. Anyone could understand these words. I quickly learned the most important reason for them...We all needed them!

So here I am, not seeking the credit as an author, writer or any such thing. I'm a simple scribe of The Master. It's not that I'm so special. It's my gift from God. I receive it and operate in it with both humility and gratitude. I desire no credit for it. My greatest desire is that everyone who reads these words see's the heart of God, and not me.

God has been extremely vulnerable and exposes His amazing heart to us through these truths He speaks. What a display of love! I stand in amazement and in humility of all of the words people say to me on how God touches their hearts through these words He gives me.

So I write as I hear. I listen always. My iPod is ever ready. Without His voice, there's only silence. I know my place as servant, and I know God's as Master. As long as He receives all the credit, all the praise and all of the attention for what He's doing, that's my greatest desire.

People have given praise to me for the gift of God within me. That's so nice of them and I appreciate their words and enthusiasm. It's only a confirmation of what God's doing, not me. For I'm a much better listener, than a writer.

We can argue with truth...But it's a fight we'll always lose!

FORWARD

C P TIME is a book of awareness not for just people of color, but for all people. There are things that we need to know about ourselves and things others should know about us. This is not a book of division but one to unite us as one people.

Prejudice stems from ignorance and the lack of understanding of a people or a person. With awareness, truth and understanding, we reach back throughout history and our races to heal, not to bring up the wrongs of our people on both sides.

CP TIME is a book which acknowledges our past for what it was but chooses to see the purpose in it, not the prejudices. The ultimate designer of our nation is and always was God. We as blacks were brought to this land for a reason. Although the method in which we arrived here was cruel, it was the same method God used for Joseph in the Bible to bring him to his place of destiny as Governor of Egypt.

For too long we've only looked at the cruelty of slavery and what was done to our people. Today, God wants us to look at the blessings that we've obtained as a people from living in this country. Here we've made vast contributions to life and society. This land is our home also, whether by choice or by destiny.

CP TIME is not a book just for and about blacks. It's a book about ourselves as people of all races. There are good and bad in all of us. There are trends in all of us that we need to address and change. Awareness brings us to these places of change. We can't change until we're first made aware of the need for change, and to grow and mature in areas of our lives as individuals and as a people.

CP TIME makes us aware of areas of faults in our lives and where we need to go to become better and to do better. Sure there are things we do collectively as races, but that doesn't make them right. If these areas are deficits within us, then we need to change them. The goal from God here is to rise as people. The goal is to stop doing wrong things expecting right results. The goal is awareness of the changes we need to make to be better people, be a better society, a better nation and a better world.

There are areas in which we need to change in life. There are trends which need to be corrected and reversed. There are ways through subtlety that have caused us to get off track from what's right. The devil will not place a big sign out saying "here's the way to sin, go this way!" He does his best work being unseen. He works through subtleties. He's at his greatest when we're unaware of what he's doing to us, the destruction he's causing and his lies we fall for.

This describes today's society. We've fallen for the subtleties and have believed wrongs were right. Instead of being aware of our ways, we've just accepted them, and our moral society has declined. Today we accept wrongs as right. Our conscience has grown silent and asleep. It must reawaken. Truth and awareness are the alarm clocks to awaken our conscience.

This book is to teach us of our past and to learn from its mistakes. It's to show a different side of our story, from the perspective of pride and purpose, no longer from bitterness, anger and resentment.

This book is meant to welcome and acknowledge the white race as our brothers and sisters in humanity and children of the same God. No one is alive today that had anything to do with the enslavement of our people. We must move on and let it go. Our white brothers and sisters today had nothing to do with the evils done to our ancestors and it's time they're released from the guilt and accusations. The people responsible are dead. It's time their ghost's no longer haunt us through bitterness and anger.

God wants peace for us all! Reach back if we must, but retreat to gain appreciation and knowledge, not bitterness, strife and hatred.

We must become more concerned with our futures...Than the bitterness of our past!

Let this book serve as a tool to teach us to never judge a man's acts by his color, but judge him for his heart. Both good and evil proceed from the same heart, regardless of the skin color of a man. Color has nothing to do with the hatred in the world. It will always stem from the heart of an individual. Knowing this, we can judge a man for his heart, not the shallowness of his color. His color isn't the culprit...It's his heart! This will prevent us from labeling and lumping blame on entire races of people. Unfortunately, we all don't represent our races well. Pride and shame come from us all.

Let these words serve as a guide, lamp, light, compass and measuring stick, to show us where we are as individuals, not as races, and where we need to improve. Let's take the focus off of race and place it on us as individuals first. Race only divides. One day we'll all stand before the throne of God and give an account for what we've done as individuals, not as members of any race. Responsibility must be a personal issue before it can become a collective one!

May the pages in this book give us a better understanding of each other. May it destroy myths, stereotypes, misconceptions and misunderstandings. May these pages serve as a bridge to join us together and no longer separate and divide us. May they serve as a guide to unite us as individuals with different shades of skin, men and women, husbands and wives, parents and children and children of One Father...God!

This is not a book for African American's; it's a book for all people. Yes, there are certain parts pertaining to us as African Americans but it's only to help others understand us and to help us understand ourselves. With understanding comes clarification, and clarification brings acceptance. We must know ourselves and others must know us, our struggles, our tragic and triumphant past, and our contributions so we can also stand as valuable and needed members of society.

But before we can be a united people of all races, we must let go of the pains and the bitterness of our past. No one alive today is responsible for the slavery our ancestors went through. Even if they were, God would still require us to forgive them. There is no moving forward without Forgiveness!

THE FACES IN THE STONE

At first only the artist can see the images in the stone. With such a colossal task, he must hire workers to become his hands. Their tools must become his paint brush. Initially, all artists that dream big are considered fools. It's only after their product is complete that these same fools become geniuses.

The artist can see the images in the stone. He must direct laborers with no experience and at times no clue, of what his vision is. The workers aren't required to see, nor even understand the artist's vision. He must simply carry out his instructions.

At first he walks in blind faith, chipping away stone at the request of the artist. He will not have the privilege of seeing nor understanding the significance of his work until sometime later.

The artist sets a plumb bob at the top of the head of the first figure. The plumb bob falls, and its point will serve as a reference to both artist and worker. The point of the plumb bob will serve as the furthest point on the face of the first figure. Nothing will go beyond that point. From the furthest point, the artist works backwards towards the face of the rock. With each blast of rock, with each chipping away of stone, a small image begins to emerge.

Only now when the worker has finished for the day, can he peer up at the face of the stone and begin to see a brief image. He begins to see the fruition of his labor. Before, it was just work. Before, he was working for a fool. Before, he was just going through the motions and following orders for a pay check. Before, he cared less if this artist was lunatic or sane. As long as he got paid, was his only concern.

An artist is often scorned. He's been given a gift from God that no one else sees. So he's mocked and ridiculed. The visionary, the dreamer moves past the scorn and opinion of others because he's been given a gift to see as only God sees. He's had a glimpse into the infinite wisdom of God. He's grateful for the privilege to see as no ordinary man sees.

He ignores the voices and opinions of others because his life has now become a mission. He's on assignment by God and he must see his work through. It drives him. It becomes his life and his energy. He pushes himself past the pain of fatigue and failure, and just as the plumb bob, stays true to his course.

After days and countless hours, the workers that became his hands, with tools which served as his brush, step down from the day's work and spends more and more time gazing up at the image which begins to form out of the mountain.

Something remarkable happens. As the workers look and see the image starting to form, their feelings and opinions begin to change towards the artist. He's no longer a fool. The specific instructions that he gave had meaning after all. He was directing the strokes of his brush through the tools in their hands.

It was all now beginning to make sense. The miracle of "buy-in" has occurred; instead of the artist being eccentric, now the workers can see his vision. The work becomes no longer just a job, but a mission. It's more than just a pay check now, it's an assignment. He's no longer just a worker taking orders; he's a part of something magnificent and colossal.

This is no ordinary painting. This is a monumental undertaking that generations to come will stand at the foot of the mountain, look up and wonder in amazement how such a task could have been accomplished. The sight never gets old. The view never fades. This is on a grand scale like nothing that's been done before. One day you too will stand at the foot of the mountain, look up and wonder in amazement how you could have been a part of something so extraordinary.

With all your complaining at first and inability to see nor understand the artist's vision, you almost missed out on a once in a lifetime opportunity. You breathe in and out again, and come back to reality and the truth. Your decision of many years ago has affected your today. You made the choice back then to persevere, when you didn't understand the direction of the artist. You walked blindly, taking orders by faith.

Yes, even you called him a fool, and said under your breath, that he didn't know what he was doing.

Today is a special day! It's a day like many others when you look back in gratitude for being blind, yet walking anyway. You stand at the foot of the mountain today and look up, and what you see are the colossal faces of four American Presidents carved in the face of the mountain, which you helped countless people stand in awe and amazement of.

You weren't just drilling away rock in the face of a mountain. You were creating a National Treasure, for all generations.

It's a testament to what ordinary men can do through an extraordinary leader or one who has tremendous vision. The visionary elevates the level of his co-worker's, they begin to see the essence of his art. Art is not something that everyone gets to be a part of. When the opportunity arises, one puts down his brushes to become a bristle in the brush of the Artist.

This artist paints not for himself, but for humanity!

Chapter 1

CP Time No More

The dirt of our Ancestors...Is the Ground we stand upon today!

Let This Book Serve
Let this book stand as a tool to unite our races. Initially we were forced to be together. That force is no longer the reason we're together. Those that did this to us are long gone. They thought not of the consequences or the residuals of their evil in forcing one race upon another against its will.

They weren't wise enough to think ahead of the destruction, the hatred and the tension it would cause between our races once the brutality ended. They didn't think that far. They didn't care! They weren't thinking of our generations. They were only thinking of theirs. There's a great lesson here. A generation that only thinks of itself will ruin the lives of the generations behind them!

The generation which started slavery were only thinking of themselves. Did they think slavery would last forever? Did they not think that a country founded upon the principles and foundation of worshipping God could continue to sin through controlling a race of people against their will? Did they not think that God would one day put an end to such cruelty? The problem is...They didn't think! They didn't think of us and the residual damage it would do to our lives. They only thought of themselves!

There was no time limit placed on slavery. There was no fore-seen end. If it had been up to them, it would have lasted forever. Unfortunately, we are the products of their actions and decisions. We were forced to live together without a choice.

Now that we're here together, let's mend some things. Now that we know it wasn't our choice but God's, to bring us here to this land to benefit and to contribute, not to work as free laborers; let's live here with peace and understanding. Let the pages of this book which God, not I have given; serve as our Memorandum of Understanding. Let it serve as our Standard Operating Procedures on how to live together with Acceptance and Understanding. May we all see clearly that we are people of destiny under the mighty hand of God and serve as an example of Unity and Peace for all nations.

May we finally get it right! May we finally know that it was the purpose of God to bring us to this land to help and enhance life here. May there finally be an understanding of that between our races. May it bring about a new understanding that all of us migrated here from somewhere else. We all were foreigners to this land at one time, yet were accepted here. None of us were natives to this land except the Indian.

Finally, may this bring with it Acceptance and no longer just tol-erance of our lives together. May the lines of tension be broken. May the walls between us be torn down. May we expand our boarders to Include, and Exclude no more.

May we be the people that finally fulfill the words of The Constitution...That All men are created equal with rights to Liberty and Justice. May this prophecy of our forefathers finally be fulfilled in us!

CP Time No More

Being a people of Excellence has nothing to do with Color, but has everything to do with Character!

Never have a people risen from such depths to such heights. Never have a people been placed in the darkest recesses of life only to rise in the light of humanity. We are the only people which have a common history of bondage with the chosen people of God... Slavery.

Our lives and our history began here in this land with a deficit; a huge deficit of depravity, bondage, abuse and neglect. For the simple pigmentation of our skin, we were deemed inferior and less human. Our stock was numbered amongst the farm animals and equipment. Never was a race of people formed and born in the image of the Almighty deemed less than whom God created them to be.

We were seen as the lowest form of humanity. We were sold and used to build a nation we lived in but wasn't a part of. We would be used in the lowest forms and ways. Our families would be broken by sales and auctions. Our women would be raped at the leisure of a slave owner. Their husbands would be left humiliated with no recourse, no action and no voice to debate the viscous act...But left to look at a child born to his wife he knew he didn't father.

Time would eventually cause us to forget our customs and the great continent from which we came. Time had given us a new home now on this once unfamiliar America. No, we wouldn't leave after the law had set us free. This land had now become our home also. We welcomed it, we believed in its Constitution to one day honor us as equal and valuable citizens as well. We would stand for our new nation, fight for it and even die for it.

This was our past. A people looked upon as low as the earth we stood upon. This was our past. This is not our present. Thanks to our ancestors who worked, studied and educated themselves through the help of others who believed that our people weren't any less than any other man than breathed, we began to rise.

Our people found ways to receive education. We weren't an unintelligent people. We just weren't given the same opportunities as others. But thanks to our ancestors with pure determination, hard work and unselfishness, we would be recognized for our contributions to humanity.

No, it wasn't easy by any means. We would have to learn under the worst conditions and receive through the back door what others could boldly receive through the front, wide opened doors. But we persevered! We were determined not to fail. Bumps, hurdles, stop signs, violence were all along our paths. Yet they wouldn't stop us, but gave us the sheer desire to press even harder for what we believed we had a right to receive.

We wanted respect too. We wanted respect for ourselves, amongst ourselves and from others. We too had much to contribute if only given the chance. History hasn't been kind enough to tell our stories, our contributions and our triumphs. So we must tell them ourselves. But not out of malice, bitterness or hatred. But out of pride for a people that has triumphed from the lowest recesses of humanity. A proud people who endured years of slavery, disrespect and put under the foot of humanity; yet would rise!

Today our people, descendants of these proud people, face our own issues. These issues unlike our ancestors can't be blamed on another race of people...But on Ourselves. What have we done with the contributions, the struggles, the sufferings, the triumphs of these great people that have risen us to our current places in life?

We've abused our rights, our privileges and the gifts given to us on the backs and stripes of our ancestors. All that they fought for, all that they struggled for, all they were beaten and bruised for and even all they died for...We have misused.

Our ancestors were full of pride because they scraped, clawed and crawled for every inch they gained in society and in humanity. We were simply handed the places in life they would never see by the sweat, blood and tears of their broken bodies. What would we do with these precious, priceless gifts? We squander them away with pride, arrogance, apathy and foolishness.

The farther we get away from God, the farther we get away from such things as thanks, appreciation, self respect, respect for others, for life and mankind. Without God, our conscience is put to sleep with apathy and we believe there's nothing wrong with what we're doing. Who cares about the past! Who cares about history! That stuff's in the past and doesn't affect my life today! That's a lie that couldn't be farther from the truth. We're a product of our histories both good and bad. It was history which introduced each one of us to life today.

As a people, we've run the gamut of being a people on "CP Time" type of people. CP Time meaning being on Colored People Time.

CP Time is an expression we use amongst ourselves for making excuses for deficits in our character and responsibilities. "I wasn't late! I was just on CP Time!" Or where's so and so? "I guess they're running on CP Time!"

Yes it's funny and we joke about these shortcomings, but there's a standard that far exceeds the CP standard, a standard that we're all held accountable to. That standard is not the CP standard of living; it's the "GP" standard of living. GP standing for God's People and People of Character!

CP Time is much more than running late, being late and not starting our programs on time. It's an attitude of mediocrity. It shows a lack of professionalism, apathy and irresponsibility. CP Time is our bad attitudes and our poor work ethics. It's how we display ourselves as a race to the world. It only perpetuates the stereotypes placed upon our people when we lower ourselves to CP Time. Who can take us serious if we're irresponsible, late and unprofessional? We have grown so accustomed to the CP standard that we just expect it as common place.

We even show up late for things as we know we won't start our events on time. A man told me yesterday that when he plans something, he adds an hour to whatever time he wants people to be there. Even then they're late he said.

We have to rise above this standard. We have to abolish it. It only makes us look bad. We constantly have to be on our "A" game and bring it.

Let CP Time become a standard of awareness for people of all races on how far we've digressed and where we need to go. Let it stand for awareness for all people because after learning what God teaches us through this book, we'll abolish its original meaning!

CP TIME NO MORE...WE CAN ILL AFFORD IT!

THEY ARE US, WE ARE THEM

They're our ancestors; those that have come and gone before us. We exist because of them. We breathe because they lived. We strive because they survived.

It was the words that echoed in their minds daily as soon as they exited from sleep and were awaken to the reality of life..."I must fight, I must survive!" After a pleasant night's sleep when the body and mind rejuvenate themselves, these are the words that arrived each morning to greet our people..."I must fight, I must survive!"

Dr. King was a gift from God to humanity. Looking back, I can see his goal; his task wasn't the same as the one of Unity that God has assigned to me. His task was narrower, more precise and specific. His task was the basic entitlements of a man living on this planet...Being recognized, appreciated, acknowledged and wanted.

Our ancestors, not even so long ago, lived in a time where they weren't even tolerated as human beings. What do such things do to a man's dignity and self esteem? To be recognized, not to be looked down upon and despised, should be basic rights all people should receive when they enter life.

The fight was there each day, each morning when our ancestors opened their eyes with the new sun. The fight was there as they struggled to find menial and degrading work just to feed and provide for their families. The fight was there when they could not sit in a bus seat or be served at a restaurant. The fight was there when just because of the shade of their skin; they were beaten or killed for no other reason than being black.

But they survived! Through tremendous heartache, turmoil and hardships, they would make it. We are the residuals of the success and survival of our ancestors. We're survivors of the strong! We're the seed of survivors. We are them! They are us, living in us and through us, as we show them the new day they never seen.

There is something we owe these great people. We owe them our strength, our gratitude and our appreciation. We owe them our strength to carry on the standards of excellence they've set for us. We owe them the fight to prove we're intellectual people of great significance and contributions.

They had to fight for what we take for granted everyday of our lives. They had to fight just to be recognized as human beings. They had to fight for education. They had to fight for their own freedoms.

Today, we are absent of any major struggles. No, things aren't perfect and we've be blessed to come far, thanks to God through men like Dr. King who gave his voice, his charisma, his intelligence, his education and sometimes even his pride and his dignity to give us rights, recognition and the acknowledgement we enjoy today.

During the times of our ancestors, who arrived here in chains and bondage, their greatest desire was freedom. One day our ancestors would become free citizens. In Dr. King's time, our people fought just to be seen, recognized and acknowledged. But before our people can ever be a people of destiny, the people that God allowed our ancestors to come to this land to be, we must look back, reach back and look at where we've come, know the struggle and the fight of our ancestors. To be a people that are truly free...We Must Forgive!

We can no longer be angry about our past. We can no longer be angry about the people in our past that did some terrible acts to our ancestors. Anger only besets us. It freezes us in a place and time. We're stuck! It requires all of our focus and energy towards wrong. We must forgive the past. We must forgive the people of the past no matter how wrong and cruel they were. If we don't, we become them.

We become no different than them. Hate will never profit any of us. To harbor bitterness for the acts done in the past to our people is just as the slavery and bondage they physically endured. The only difference is the slavery of un-forgiveness and bitterness is self inflicted. This is slavery we place ourselves in. It's a self imposed absence of freedom. Its freedom we steal from ourselves. We'll have no one to blame but ourselves.

Forgiveness is the mandate of God and His requirement for advancement. Thanks to the sacrificial life of Dr. King and so many others, we've been acknowledged with the basic rights of mankind. Now each of us stands as individuals before the door placed before us, to determine if we'll open or close it. We do this with our attitudes, our dispositions, our anger or our forgiveness. We do this by

25

acknowledging and remembering our ancestors and all they suffered and survived to give us better and proper lives.

We do this by being them and allowing them to live through us with their spirits of determination and tenacity. We do this by never giving up, by showing up on time, by being exceptional and by not allowing the extremely high standards they set never falter is us one iota.

Through time our people have gone through ages. Initially it was the age of just obtaining our freedom. Then it was the age of acknowledgement, being recognized as human beings and contributors. Now that we've been recognized, somewhat accepted, and not just tolerated, God is moving us into the age of Unity.

Acceptance and appreciation must precede Unity. It's only then can we be one people under God with no division in regards to race. It's only then that the words penned in The Constitution will finally be fulfilled.

Chapter 2

A Proud People

~~

The rights and freedoms of man are not up to the dictation of man…
But by the mandate of God, his creator!

AFRICA HAS COME TO AMERICA

W e weren't invited, but were brought by force, with chains
around our wrists and ankles. We were brought here against
our will. What did you think you would do to us when your laws
would no longer keep us as slaves? We had minds too. We were
blessed with intelligence. There was genius within us also. We could
only be kept down for so long.

A man can only contain the thoughts in his mind for so long,
eventually they must be released. A man's intellect can only be sti-
fled for so long. Eventually his ideas must be expressed, pursued
and acted upon.

This is why God gave them to him. Not for him to take his gifts
with him to the grave, but to express them while he lives. Ideas
in the mind are meant to be products and inventions to further the
development of mankind.

We no longer know the land from which we came. We've lost
any relations we have there. We've adopted this land which you've
brought us to as our home. We were people you hated after you
brought us here. Imagine being despised only for your color.

Even when you made it illegal for us to receive an education, we found a way. Your goal may have been to keep us ignorant, but it wasn't God's plan for us. Your plan for us may have been to work your lands for free, but God had other ideas for us. Just as Joseph was taken from his family and sold into slavery, so were we. The path of slavery was only part of Joseph's life. Slavery would only be a part of our lives. Where God needed Joseph was in Egypt. God needed us here!

We no longer know the land we came from, nor the people that gave us life. In the big scheme of things, we weren't brought here, but sent to this land by God. What if it were true? Could we remember, but also let go of some things. Could we let go of some hurts from yesterday and move forward with our purpose for tomorrow? Is it not the will of God to live peaceably with all men? Was it not the dream of Dr. King to live in harmony with all races? Isn't it time for resentment to be over? We're no longer Africans, but African Americans.

If given the opportunity to speak the truth, you would see that God has done great and magnificent works through us as well. You'll see that even on the back of slavery, the lowest condition for a human being, we rose to prominence. Not just because of opportunities given, but because of what was in us could not be contained. We were given to give, born to contribute. Like Joseph, our destiny was in another land.

Our races have been blended. None of us are completely African anymore. We are a different race now, one in which your men helped to created. You despised our men but not our women. We are a people that have been knocked down, yet have stood. We are people that have been pressed down, but would rise. Don't ask us to forget our past; our past is who we are.

A man that doesn't know his past is a man that doesn't know who he is. It's the struggles and the triumphs that produce character within a race. We are an "in spite of," a "regardless of" people. We have stood amidst the tremendous pressure of fire hoses, biting dogs and imprisonment. We were hated only because we were different. Difference is what makes the world a better place; a more expanded and exciting place, where every man contributes with the gifts of God within him.

If we were to look in our Bibles, we would see the truth about some very important things. One, we would see that life began for the very first seeds of life in Africa. Adam was given life on what is now the continent of Africa. Another thing we would find in the Bible is there were people whom the Egyptians feared, because their numbers we so large. They feared they would overtake them, so they fought them and turned them into slaves. Without knowing the complete story, we could feel sorry for these people. But these weren't just any people; they were the children of Israel. These were God's chosen people.

To be chosen by God is a privilege, not a curse! These people, God's own chosen people, endured the harshness of slavery for hundreds of years. Yet they were still the chosen people of God. Slavery did not diminish that. Sometimes it's not the condition a man finds himself in that defines him. It's the eyes in which he sees himself through. It's whose eyes a man is found in that matters...In the All Seeing Eyes of God.

Even through the hard times, the pain and the suffering, their status didn't change. They were still the chosen of God. Chosen people or not, God allowed these people to be taken as slaves. There is nothing in life that God can't prevent if He chooses. When He chooses not to intervene, there is a bigger reason than we can see. God is sovereign and incapable of making mistakes.

Let's look at another people. These people were also from the continent of Africa. These people were Africans. Whether due to their numbers, their culture or whatever it was, these people were also taken into slavery. They, like the children of Israel, endured the cruelties of slavery and much worse. Even after the Constitution of this great nation, penned by men who believed in God, stated that "All men are created equal," the laws of this nation would not support its own Constitution. Once the laws were finally changed, what was left was prejudice and injustice for these people.

Even years after the law had been changed to free a people, they still weren't free. These were only ghost words like "coincidence" and "luck." They had no true meaning or substance. It was like a sugar pill given to a hypochondriac. A placebo of truth is still a lie.

These people lived in a placebo of freedom. The letter of the law told them they were free, but the words and actions of man told them otherwise. Yet they endured for years under such illusions. Amidst laws that prevented them from receiving an education, they found ways.

My uncle J. R. Clifford wasn't allowed to attend law school, but with only reading law books in an attorney's office, took and passed the West Virginia state bar exam to become the states first Black attorney. Pride amongst a people finds a way to succeed.

Going back to the Bible, we see that although the children of Israel were made slaves, they weren't cursed; they were the chosen people of God. Looking at our own race, whose been called cursed and every other name in the book, I see through the wisdom of God, that although our past is horrid, we are not a cursed people...But a blessed people! We too have been taken from our land like Joseph and the nation of Israel, but it was all for a purpose larger than ourselves.

Look at the lives we live today. Look at all we've been given and been blessed with. We live in the greatest nation on earth and we helped to build it with the sweat and tears of our ancestors. Although it was horrible, slavery brought us to this land. It wasn't a curse. It was our destiny to be the people we are today. It was an allowance by God. It gave us spiritual roots that were dug strong and deep into the ground. We worshiped God with enthusiasm and passion, for He was all we had. Our songs rose up from within our hearts and our struggles, and were sung with pain as well as hope. These songs kept us strong through adversity. Our struggles kept us dependent on God.

From God's point of view, these are people that He uses to do great things. Humility and brokenness are tremendous gifts overlooked by many. But they are the necessary gifts which God needs in a people to serve Him and not themselves.

So we thank the few that made us many today. We thank the many that have made us few, a few people that will see that the "God allowed" struggles of our past will produce humility within us today. A few that will stand up, not in malice, but in remembrance, that our struggles have given us character, not hate. A few that will see our horrid past only as stepping stones to greatness in our lives and in our destinies. A few that will remember as well as forget, forgive and move forward with life, letting nothing or no one hold them down.

In forgiveness there is freedom. In reality there is truth. The truth is for some reason, God allowed our ancestors to be taken as slaves.

I choose to see that in a better light, not a bitter one. I choose to see that from a spiritual insight, not my own, which can only cause anger within me. I choose to see that God wanted a better life for us and we all have it now. I choose to see that without our past, I wouldn't know who I am today. A man is defined by his past, by those that went before him. A man can never know who he is until he knows where he comes from.

I wouldn't have had the opportunity through birth, to know God. Would any of us even have been born that live here today? Just think about it!

Let this be the time for healing on both sides, the user and the used, the victim and the victimizer, the abuser and the abused, the culprit and the recipient. This is not the time to forget theses acts, but to remember them, so they'll never be repeated. Remember them and pass them on so others can see the mistakes of the past and learn from them.

But let this be a time for peace, for forgiveness and unity. A man can never move forward while being stuck in his past. Let the wrongs of the past give us all wisdom for today and tomorrow. Let it be time!

Let this be clear to all men, that God was not involved in the act of slavery of any race of people. Slavery was born out of the evil heart of man. It would be ended by the Hand of God. It was evil in every sense. It was the evil intent of man, which God Himself eventually turned around for good.

God would see that through this vicious act of cruelty, that there would be immeasurable contributions through the Black race for the benefit of the Human Race.

FROM THE LEAST TO GREATNESS

Because the start of our lives here began in slavery, at life's lowest form, we have always had to prove we were intelligent and gifted people who could make significant contributions to life and society. It's what our proud ancestors started. It's what we must continue even in today's times.

Dating back to the Revolutionary and Civil War's, we've had to prove ourselves worthy to fight and could be trusted to fight for what we also believed in. If we were only given a chance, we could exceed the standards established for us. Had the regiment from Massachusetts not demonstrated extraordinary service in the Civil War, there would be no "Glory" to exhibit the qualities and sacrifices of these brave soldiers. The Tuskegee Airmen was an experiment. People didn't believe our ancestors had the intelligence to fly aircraft. Our people had to fight for the right just to fight in wars past.

What if Benjamin O. Davis and the men of Tuskegee didn't take this project serious? What if they did just enough to get by? Just getting by is not the standard for Excellence, and in times to prove yourself as a people or a race. Doing more than required is the only standard that is acceptable during such times. These men knew that. They knew they would only get one shot to prove themselves with hand me down equipment and planes. Yet the success of our generations rested upon their shoulders and their success.

The story plays like a record. Throughout history our people have had to do more with less to be considered almost equal. There was no room for letdown nor lessened efforts. We had to be the best. We had to stand out in the most positive ways. We had to take what was given to us and take it higher, faster and further.

In wartime, the Tuskegee Airman would develop such a reputation for excellence in bomber escort, that they became requested by white bomber pilots. They painted the tails of their planes with a bright red color to distinguish themselves to both friend and foe. To friend, they were a welcomed sight. To the enemy, they were an unfortunate sight. These men were on a mission to destroy all enemy aircraft and to protect the bombers they were assigned to escort.

They exceeded the standards expected of them. They lost many of their own men, but never lost a single bomber they protected. That's a phenomenal accomplishment and probably one never repeated.

The men of the 333rd Field Artillery fought behind the front lines in the Battle of the Bulge and WWII protecting our troops fighting on the front lines. These men were so proficient with their 155 Howitzer weapon that YANK Magazine highlighted these black soldiers in an article in September of 1944 in a segregated Army.

The 333rd took out a German Tiger tank killing our troops on the front lines from nine miles away. On another occasion, the troops on the front lines were having a problem with a sniper taking out our troops from a church steeple. The call was sent to the 333rd. One round was launched taking out the target from three miles away. The 555th with its tank division was called into action by General Patton and performed their duties beyond expectations.

These are just a few of the many untold stories of our black troops exemplary service to our nation during critical times in our history which demonstrated not only our abilities, but our contributions to preserve this free nation we live in today. I was told of a story of a black outfit working on a road in Alaska. They were given the worst equipment and very little support. Not only did they complete the road by improvising and pure ingenuity, they completed their work way ahead of schedule. Many of them died doing this, yet it was a sacrifice they were willing to make to prove themselves.

Proof in a person or a people never come without great cost and sacrifice!

The point here is just because we live in today's times with various freedoms and privileges, doesn't mean we can rest on our laurels and not continue the high standards our people set for us. There would be little privileges today for us if our ancestors had not exceeded the standards of yesterday. We have a duty and an obligation to exceed and excel at all things we do as individuals and as a people.

Eyes are still watching us. That's not a bad thing. If anything, it should cause us to step up and keep the Standard of Excellence those before us set. We have the obligation to continue this standard.

CITIZENS OF SURVIVORS

We all came from someone, from somewhere. It was our ancestors that endured, survived and made it for us to carry on the tremendous pride, customs and heritage they once practiced. It's not our
place to forget them. These things define us.

They're in our blood deep within us. They're the strength of us,
the pride, the courage, the determination and the life of us. Without
knowing this, we'll be lost. We're not a new race. We're a race of
our ancestors. We carry them within us. We must never forget this
fact.

Where do we find ourselves as a race of people with its origin
from the large continent of Africa? This is our heritage. These are
our roots. From Africa is where we originated as a people. We were
a proud, intelligent people living and thriving on the continent where
life began.

Let's move forward in time. Slavery comes and strips us of our
homes, our customs, our families, our traditions, our freedom and
our dignity. For hundreds of years, our people entered and exited
life in bondage as slaves. Eventually, all original Africans would die
off through time.

Time could take away the lives, but could not reduce the pride in
the people. We were a strong people who survived the worst that life
would thrust upon us. We weren't meant to be kept under the foot
of man, but instead we rose to survive the punishments and cruelties of the times in which we lived. We endured through the greatest
of hardships, disappointments, discouragements and degradations.
We're a strong people and we survive.

God is never ignorant nor unaware of the plans of man on earth.
There is never the slightest minute detail that He doesn't have control over. For some reason, God allowed His chosen people Israel to
become slaves. For some reason, God allowed our people from the
same continent to become slaves on a different continent.

The plans and the purpose of God are never for evil, but for
good. Although our ancestors paid the horrible price as slaves, we
their offspring have reaped the rewards of their labor and sufferings.
For example, look at the lives we live here in America. We live on

the richest continent on earth. We enjoy liberties, freedoms and life-styles that people in Africa today don't have. We've been blessed beyond our comprehension. Don't believe this? Go visit another country overseas and see the conditions in which they live. We complain here with not having this or that, but take the time to be with children in other countries living in poverty not knowing where their next meal is coming from. We're blessed!

Look at the contributions made to this nation as a result of our people being here. From the first open heart surgery, to the traffic light, to farm machinery that helped to expand the agricultural industry; we've been major contributors in this society. This nation has benefited from the genius of our people in countless ways.

On the backs of slavery, our people struggled to receive education and become significant members of society. It was a struggle, when those with other plans for us, desired to keep us ignorant and unlearned. But thank God our ancestors wouldn't stand for this and pushed forward anyways. Thank God there were good people on the other side of the struggle with opportunities and compassion.

When the laws didn't cooperate with giving them an education, our people found ways to be educated. They weren't given an education as our children are today...They had to take an education.

In the pages of the Howard High Colored School year book, I see children and adults with picket signs marching for better schools. It was my grandfather James R. Coleman Sr. that purchased the permit to march and designed the signs held high through the towns of Piedmont and Keyser protesting for better school conditions. Howard High School would produce the likes of WWII and Battle of the Bulge Hero and one of The Wereth Eleven Soldier's, Mr. James "Aubrey" Stewart. Don Redman, the famous jazz musician who wrote and performed the music for the famous cartoon Betty Boop, also graduated from Howard High. Don Redman would go on to write for the likes of Bing Crosby, the Dorsey Brothers and conduct for Pearl Bailey and many others.

Our children have no idea of what our people had to go through just to receive something they complain about getting everyday for free...An Education! How far we've come, but what we haven't brought forward with us is...Appreciation!

Chapter 3

We Must Reach, Not Settle

It's in darkness that the brilliance of the stars shines their brightest and refuses to be hidden!

CONTENT

We must only be content that our work is no more and we are no longer a part of a contributing society, when our names have been called from on high. Then and only then can we afford to rest from our labors.

Until then, we will always have a place in the world to contribute whether that contribution is a word of wisdom or just a smile.

THE FOOLISHNESS OF NOAH

How dare this man believe he heard the voice of God! The audacity of this man to believe he heard what he heard from God. Not just to build a ship, but an ark?

What's an ark? Was he even a ship builder? Did he have the skills or the experience to build a ship? Was this his occupation? Besides, he was only Jim's boy from down the way. What about his family, his wife, when he came home one day and told her God instructed him to build an ark?

What's an ark she probably wondered? Why you? Are you sure you heard correctly concerning this? This is a huge and magnificent task, have you missed the Word of God somewhere?

Where will this ark be going? Why must we be the ones to build it? Where's the money coming from? There's work I've been asking you to do around this house for months that you've neglected, now this ridiculous ark building has consumed your every moment!

What about his neighbors? They say "Noah's really lost it this time!" Look at that foolish monstrosity he's building. For what? He and his family are fools for building such a ship so far from sea.

The laughter, the ridicule, the mockery, it all seemed appropriate...Until The Rain Came!

SOMETIMES THE ONLY THING THAT SEPARATES THE FOOL FROM THE GENIUS...IS SUCCESS!

If you've heard the voice of God in your heart to pursue a task, a career or a dream, know that just like Noah, the critics will come. They'll come to discourage, to disrupt and to down grade what you've heard, and what direction you believe God is calling you. Your dreams are between you and the One who gave them...God. Pursued, you could do something as foolish as Noah...and save the world!

As the first earth rain descends and your ark begins to float... Fool no more, fool no more!

WE CAN'T AFFORD TO REST...KEEP THE BAR RAISED HIGH!

The bar was raised high by our ancestors. It had to be. It was the only way they were allowed to participate and contribute...by exceeding the standards which were set before them. They couldn't just meet the standard. Meeting it wasn't enough for our people. We had to go beyond what we were required to do. We had to do it better and more efficiently. We weren't part of the world of just getting by. The only way we received opportunities was by doing more than was expected of us. Our ancestors were afforded few opportunities. They had to make the best of each of them!

Today we may live in different times, but that standard set by our ancestors still applies to us today. They knew they had to do more, had to be better as a race to be afforded opportunities. Not that we don't have our fair share of opportunities, it's what we do with them that counts. Do we squander them or make the best of them? Do we think of the ones coming behind us as well?

There is one important lesson we sometimes overlook, we not only work for ourselves, but we work for the generations behind us. Just as our ancestors did, we must do also. We must continue the high standards set for us to excel and not be content with just doings enough to get by. Had it not been for the standards they set in their times, we would not have the opportunities in ours. It was on the back of Jackie Robinson that broke the colored barrier in major league baseball. He didn't get there because he was mediocre. He got there on his work ethic.

Even today in our opportunistic times, we can I'll afford to let that bar be lowered one inch. It must be raised. It must stay raised. We too must unselfishly think of the opportunities we'll leave for our children and the generations behind them. We must shine, to continue to afford them opportunities and chances as our ancestors have done for us.

We have not arrived! We can't afford to rest on our laurels. We can't afford the slightest let up. We still must prove ourselves today; not to a man nor a race of men, but to God and society. The requirement is really from Him. Whatever we do, we are to do unto God and He doesn't want our seconds. He wants our best. Doing unto God is the highest standard on earth.

By pleasing Him, by rising to the expectations of meeting His standards, we can't help but be exceptional in whatever we do. Wanting to do our best unto God will have a outstanding residual effect on the work that we do for company, corporation or man.

GOOD WASN'T GOOD ENOUGH

Starting life here in America with a deficit would only cause our people to have to work hard to destroy the stereotypes placed upon us. Without given a chance, we were deemed lazy, shiftless, unintelligent, and untrustworthy. How could all of these stereotypes come simply because of the color of our skin? Someone had to make them up and someone had to convince a lot of people they were true.

Our people didn't come from the jungles in Africa like I saw in those Tarzan movies when I was a child. They came from thriving communities and societies. What people wouldn't appear ignorant and unintelligent after being snatched from their homes and brought in chains to a land they never heard of to do something they knew nothing of? These people were completely out of their element, not to mention a land, a society, a culture, a language and a continent they never heard of.

They knew their language, not English. They knew their food, their culture and their customs, not the ones of this land. After all, they weren't being offered jobs here, they were being forced to work jobs or beaten unto submission for their abstinence. They had no choice and no say so in the matter. It was work or the whip.

Unfortunately, this was our beginning here. No other race of people came here with steel wrapped around their bodies. When our freedom came, with that came the new and permanent standard for our lives and for our people.

In the workplace we would have to prove ourselves just to be paid less and to work in the worst conditions. This didn't stop nor deter our people. They were descendants of survivors. By the time their freedom came hundreds of years later, all of the original Africans had died off and those remaining would be born here in America, which was the only home they knew.

They really had no lives to return to in Africa. What was not passed down was lost and the traces of their ancestry faded as the setting of the sun. Who remained that knew the towns and villages they came from? Who remembered the languages and the customs of their original ancestors that were forced to come to this land as free labor? All that knew the places, the names, the languages, the customs, eventually died off. Those that remained, now a changed people, born and bred in this land, the only land they ever knew as home; would call this home.

Once their freedom came, so did the standard. Because others wrongly taught that our people were lazy, shiftless, irresponsible and unintelligent, this stereotype didn't die, but would be passed down through the generations. So to disprove these misconceptions our people had to raise their standard of living, keep it raised and constantly display it.

Mediocre would never work for us, and rightfully so. We were far better than middle of the road. Being good wasn't good enough. Great wouldn't even cut it. We had to be Exceptional & Extraordinary! This was our standard just to be recognized and given a chance. This is who and what we had to be just to get our foot in the door. There was no room for slacking, goofing off or missing a beat. This was our standard to not only survive, but to thrive in this America. But we were up for the challenge. We were determined to prove those wrong that mislabeled us. We wouldn't do this by force or violence, but with intelligence and pure determination.

What one did, stood for us all. We moved forward and excelled on the backs of success of one of us at a time. This was no easy road by any means. It was brutal, hard work. Determination always is. But this is the blood from which we came, those determined not just to survive, but to thrive wherever their new lives existed.

The bar has been raised high by our ancestors. That bar is a unmoveable bar, never to be lowered even in our time. The standard still remains for our people. It may not be as noticeable, but we're the descendants of slaves and we must always break the mold of stereotype upon our race. We don't do this out of malice, pride, bitterness or vengeance; we do it with intelligence, a dynamic work ethic and a solid character.

Yes, we've obtained much today. And no, it was not us who obtained it. It was the work ethic of our ancestors and their success one day, one breath and one life at a time. We owe them to never let that bar lower one inch. It's because of them that we have our nice careers, fancy cars and beautiful homes.

Had they been lazy, had they been shiftless, had they been unintelligent, had they been irresponsible and conformed to the stereotypes placed upon them as fact not fiction, it could very well be possible that we would be seen today as they were back then...Only good as entertainers, cooks, and cleaning house.

The next time you think about slacking, the next time you think about doing just enough to get by, read this chapter and snap out of selfishness. We each have an obligation, not only to ourselves and to each other, but to the generations behind us. Our ancestors did it for us. They raised us to the lofty stages we stand upon today. A generation thanks the generation before them by keeping the bar raised for the ones behind them.

Keep the bar raised high and never let it fall...Not Even One Inch!

Chapter 4

Dr. King's Sacrifice

None of us will be remembered for selfish lives...We'll be remembered for being the ones content on living our lives for the enhancement of others!

THERE WAS A MAN

There was a man, an intelligent man who excelled at all he did. In college, he graduated at the top of his class. He was a talented, gifted man, blessed with many attributes. He was blessed with charm, charisma and he was a dynamic orator.

He would use his talents, not for himself but for others. He was married and had four children. He had a beautiful wife who would always stand by his side. This was no ordinary man; this man was chosen by God. He was chosen for a cause far greater than himself.

A man chosen by God doesn't have much to say about it. His cause is the reason for his birth. He was placed on this earth to affect the lives of others for good. Yes, he may wrestle with this calling. He may not understand it at times. He may even run from it. But in the end, God gets His man. That man comes to know why he lives. So it was with this special man. He accepted the reason that he lived. He accepted the call of God upon his life.

He was endowed with gifts that would assist him in completing his task. He was well liked and respected. Just to look at him, you knew he was special. But to hear him speak...You knew he was chosen!

He would champion a cause for humanity. He would fight without swords or violence. His weapon of choice was his voice, truth, awareness and intelligence. He would move the masses. He would gather millions. He would serve as the General of the people who had been promised, but never fulfilled.

At an early stage in his life, he would decide this was why he was born, to champion the needs of others. He was a very unselfish man. He would do this in spite of his wife and children that he loved dearly. He would do this at the risk of his families and his own safety. He would do this at the risk of dying an early death.

He would be arrested, not for the wrongs a man usually does... but for Rights! With his character, intellect, conscience and heart, he would never be one even to see the inside of a jail cell. Yet he did, for others.

He risked being arrested for what he believed in. This is a man that truly stands for his cause, when he risks being finger printed and having his mug shot taken for what he believes in. He would pay the price that came with his calling.

He fought for rights he wouldn't see himself. He risked it all! He would take a stand for injustice simply because it was the right thing to do. He saw his future, yet he continued to press forward for the rights of others anyway. He knew the consequences. All heroes do.

He would change the lives of countless millions that he would never see. His mission still lives on. His voice is still heard resoundingly. He still is the voice of the people, for the people.

He had a dream of peace. He dreamed of rights and equality for all people. He was the youngest man to ever win the Nobel Prize for Peace. He was the Champion of the Cause, for rights of not just his people, but all people. He took a stand. He knew the odds. Yet he stood anyway.

At some point in our lives we'll be asked to take a stand for what we believe in. When that day comes, may we believe in humanity as a whole, and not for self, or self kind. When that day comes may we stand for the rights of all people, instead of the rights for only a select few. May we also honor the code that standing for what's right takes both sacrifice and commitment. May we stand in spite of the cost; He did!

He was our man, the Man of the People; A man for all people. Today and always he will stand for Hope & Freedom For All. His Light has never grown dim...It Never Will!

He was the Reverend Doctor Martin Luther King Jr. The body of Dr. King may have died, but the man, the motivator, the Champion of the People, the Timeless Legacy, The Obedient Man of God, The Dreamer and The Dream...No bullet could ever quench nor silence!

DR. KING'S SACRIFICE

Did Dr. King sacrifice his life for us to hold on to the hurts and pains of our past and to let un-forgiveness rob us of our true freedoms?

Un-forgiveness is one of the easiest and most popular ways Satan keeps us bound, immature, powerless, stuck and unable to move forward in our Christian walks.

No matter how free we are or aren't in our external lives, we will never experience real freedom until it comes from within our individual hearts through forgiveness and letting go of bitterness and the pains of both our ancestor's and our own lives. Until then, freedom will always be an illusion for us.

The Emancipation Proclamation didn't give us freedom, the sacrificial death of Jesus Christ on the cross did! Our freedom isn't tied to a document; it's tied to an event; the Death, Burial and Resurrection of Jesus Christ.

Countless slaves died free, although their lives were bound to chains and tragedy. They died free because the chains of slavery may have restricted their bodies, but couldn't restrict their hearts and minds where true freedom lives. They wouldn't allow it.

True freedom has little to do with the external forces around us. True freedom has everything to do with the positions of our hearts. The change must begin in our hearts before it can take place in our minds. Our hearts and minds are linked. The deeds done in the heart are acted out through the mind.

The first step for all of us begins in the mirror. He or she is our path to freedom, as well as our only hindrance. That person we see is the benefit or the blame for the freedoms we enjoy or lack in our lives.

Yes, we thank God for the Emancipation Proclamation and the Civil Rights Act, but our freedom came long before the birth of the men that penned such documents. Our freedom came from God through Christ.

So, as of this day we are no longer without the words, wisdom and revelation knowledge from God concerning our freedom. As of this day, God will no longer accept any excuse from us to hold on to the bitterness of our past. No matter how painful...We must let it go!

As of this day, we are without excuse to be a people of anger, a confrontational people and a loud people trying to scare and bully people into giving us what we want and need. The truth is, we don't really scare or intimidate anyone. People only acquiesce to our demands to get us to be quiet, to keep us from making a scene or to remove themselves from our presence. This is not relationship... Its only tolerance! We must never ask our neighbor why so and so doesn't want to be around us. We must ask our mirrors!

Confrontation, noise and attitude have nothing to do with diplomacy. They have nothing to do with the ways of God. They are really subtle tricks and traps of Satan to keep us focused on the wrong issues so we'll never be free. It's power through un-exposure. It's strongholds by hiding truth from us. As long as the truth remains hidden; lies rule, remain and guide us. The solution to any of our problems is Truth.

What would Dr. King think if he were able to come back in time to see what he gave his life for. Sure he would be proud of the many accomplishments that not only our people have made, but the accomplishments of all people.

He would be proud to see that this nation has elected its first African-American President. But after a while, his pride would slide into disappointment, not for what others are doing to us, but for what we're doing to ourselves. He would see the anger and rage within us. He would see our inability to let go of the hurts and pains of our past.

He would see what we've done with tremendous potential and the gifts we've received from God. He would turn on a sporting event and the camera would show our players making millions of dollars yet arriving at the game in jeans, a t-shirt and a baseball cap turned sideways or backwards. Where's the pride in our appearance? What example are we setting for others, including our youth?

If we want the respect of the world, we must first show respect within ourselves. We've been deceived as a race. Today the world goes along with our styles and traditions as cool. Our race now sets the standard for what's hip and new.

We've been deceived! What we've believed as strength has been some of our greatest weaknesses. Our young men believe that strength is in fighting and physical violence. They're paying the price for their ignorance today by filling the prison cells. They were deceived into believing strength was playing with the minds and emotions of young women and leaving them to bare children they would father but wouldn't be a dad to. They neglected to see that true strength is in being responsible for our actions and taking responsibility for the children we produce in this life. Weakness is demonstrated through neglect, through running away and abandoning our responsibilities rather than facing them. They've become the fathers of the fatherless and are becoming so more and more each day.

Our young women have been deceived. They've believed a lie. They run around telling the world that they're "Strong Black Women!" Well what does that mean? True strength is not demonstrated in force, but sometimes the restraint of it.

What have you done to make yourself so strong? Have you lived through the horrors of slavery? Have you watched your husband being sold to a slave owner in another state? Have you lived through a life of bigotry, prejudice and hatred and experienced the pain of fire hoses turned on full blast to deprive you of your skin, your ability to stand and your dignity? Have you ever run from police dogs turned loose to attack you? From where have you derived your strength?

Strength comes from traumatic events we survive in life. Strength comes from standing and taking a stand. Strength comes from standing for others instead of ourselves. There's no selfishness in strength!

Their definition of strength is skewed. True strength displays sacrifice, not getting what one wants. Manipulation is not strength. Manipulation is getting what we want through coercion or demands. Only one person wins through manipulation. Manipulation is selfish.

Today many women believe being a strong woman is the ability to win all the arguments by talking loud, acting out, rolling their heads, hands on their hips and waving a finger in a person's face. That could be further from the truth. Strength is exhibited through control and restraint, not through outburst.

Arguing is a display of weakness rather than strength. Arguing is the point of losing control of our emotions and displaying them loudly and forcefully upon another. When a conversation has reached the stage of argument, we're only concerned about one person's opinions and needs...Our own! Arguing is a poor solution to problem solving. It's a two sided event with only one winner. Let's learn as the Bible says to "Come and let us reason together." To reason is to see the sides of both parties and to come up with a solution beneficial to both.

God is not buying the "I'm Strong" routine from us. He's not impressed with it at all! God is impressed with Humility and turning over our will to Him. He knows as long as we labor in our own devices, we'll be weak and deceived. If we want to see an exhibition of true strength no matter man or woman, we must look to Christ.

He possessed it all, gave it all, sacrificed it all, delivered Himself completely, laid it all down, gave His life entirely, and left the beauty of Paradise to give us life with awareness to the deceit and subtle tricks of Satan. Yes, all of this goes contrary to the world, but we're called to be a Contrary to the World Kind of People. We're not called to blend in. We're called to stand out!

Be careful what you say and how you see yourself as strong. God has His ways of exposing our true natures and believe me, you won't be who you thought you were. When God shines the light of truth upon our lives, all's we'll see is our wretched selves. Humility is what Jesus displayed; strength through humility. We can never be strong in arrogance and the lack of control of our bodies and emotions.

The world has tricked us into believing that what we see on TV is cool and we've imitated it. We've fallen for the world's version of what's right and how to live. Those ways and lifestyles are contrary to what God has called us to be. Truth is cool. A gentle spirit and a contrite heart is pleasing to God.

We must display what's right before the world, not having the world telling us how to live and act. That's backwards. We're to be both light and salt to the world. Our lights have grown dim and our salt has lost most of its flavor from blending in and not standing out; not being a peculiar people as we were called to be. The world must see different to be different. They must see the change is us before they can know they're in need of change in their own lives.

Dr. King would be proud of some things he'd see if he were allowed to come back today. But there are so many things he would find displeasing. Like the length of our pants that hang down past our knees. What image are we presenting to the world? He would be disappointed in the lack of respect we exhibit for ourselves, our elders and to the world. He would be disappointed at what we display on TV under the auspice of entertainment.

We display pure arrogance on national television and attempt to pass it off as entertainment and showmanship. We show little restraint, little respect for ourselves and very little concern for the millions of people watching. What message are we sending to the world while the camera shows our people arguing with the coaches on the sideline? What message are we sending by entertaining the crowd before we cross the end zone for a touchdown, when our only job was to score? What message are we sending? Our grandparents and great grandparents fought to discredit the stereotype others placed on us as only "Entertainer's, Cooks and House Cleaners." Are we helping or hindering all they fought for, to see us as intellectuals and significant contributors to life and society?

I wonder what Dr. King would say today if he could see what we're doing with all he sacrificed for us? Would he say, "You mean I died for this?" "You mean I sacrificed so much for our people, for them to use the lowest adjective in the world used by others to describe our people, that we hated so much, and now we're calling ourselves these words...Niggas and Pimps?" "I sacrificed my marriage, my life with my beautiful wife Coretta and my children, for our race to fight amongst ourselves, killing ourselves and showing little concern or gratitude for the many others that marched and were slain for the freedoms of our people?" "Did I really die for this?"

Dr. King was God's man. He was the mouthpiece of God. He was the Moses of his generation called to free and deliver a people in bondage. He didn't choose this task. It was chosen for him before his birth.

He accepted the task. He would give his all to the calling upon his life. He would follow it regardless of what it cost him. He would stay on the path regardless of what shook him. He would stay the course in the face of great danger to his own life and his families. He would become a martyr for justice for the rights of all people. He paid the ultimate price for us. Is this how we repay him?

THE VOICE OF THE PEOPLE

Look at how our struggles in the past joined us together as one. Look at how our many privileges today separate us. In prosperity we isolate ourselves. Through struggles we unite as one. Look at how we were united as a people during Dr. King's time. Look at how we've gone our own individual ways since he's been gone. It's the "I've got mine, you get your own" mentality!

Look at the images our youth are presenting to the world. Image is everything especially to a prospective employer. What images are our youth presenting through their packaging, through their external wrapping and attitudes? They may be impressing each other but they're not impressing prospective employers, who could affect their futures with employment and careers. How we carry ourselves says a lot about us. How we dress speaks volumes without words. First impressions are sometimes the only ones we get!

There's no longer "The Man" to blame. No, things aren't perfect and aren't always where they need to be, but they've come a long way thanks to the sacrifices of Dr. King and others who marched, picketed, put aside violence and were put in jail for our freedoms. We've become enemies to ourselves. We're destroying ourselves from within. The destruction; we can only blame on ourselves!

We will never be a strong people, we will never be a people worthy or deserving of emulation, we will never become the right voice of the people...Until we diligently seek Truth and Welcome It!

Chapter 5

Moving Forward

You'll never change a man's color...So you have to work on his heart!

LETTING GO OF THE ANGER

There have been some horrific events that have happened to our people; beginning with slavery on up to the Civil Rights movement. Our people have endured what others can't imagine.

Who knows how many of our ancestors who became ill, or frustrated of their new found loss of freedom, who were just thrown over the ship and became food for sharks. Who could stomach some of the photos of a back raised with scars from lashings, or the total disrespect of a man's neck bent with his face uncovered while hanging from a tree from his neck.

All of them are horrible images that we must not forget, but they are images and events that we must let go of our anger for. Letting go is not a sign of weakness, but strength. Letting go is not saying that it's alright, because it wasn't and never will be. Letting go is required of us by God and a perquisite for moving forward in our lives.

We can't condemn others we walk amongst today for crimes they didn't commit. We've placed our anger on the innocent. We've thrown a blanket over an entire race and have been enraged with what their ancestors did, not those presently living amongst us. Even in those times when the vicious deeds were done, it was not an entire race doing them, but select people filled with hate.

There were whites that hated slavery just as much as we did. In spite of what a society does in a period of time, there is one thing that we always must remember...God is always on the throne and He always has His people in places looking out for and standing up for the injustices of the world.

Let's face it; the deeds done to our people were horrendous. But God doesn't give any of us the right to hold on to the anger of our past nor the past of our ancestors. Living with un-forgiveness in our hearts leads to anger, anger leads to rage, rage leads to violence, and violence spreads as a result of anger that's not dealt with. The truth is, we can't afford to carry the anger someone did to us earlier today, let alone in our past or in the past lives of our ancestors.

Carrying anger causes us to shrink as individuals. We shrink to the lack of character found in the perpetrators through revenge, pay back and throwing a blanket over an entire race of people. Our rage is directed towards an entire race rather than singling out wrong individuals and dealing with them for what they've done, not the race they represent. The fact is, we all don't represent our races in the best ways. There's good and bad in all of us.

Today, we're in a bondage just as bad as slavery. That bondage is called Anger & Un-forgiveness. Our ancestors may have been bound with chains, but their hearts, minds and spirits could never be contained. They were survivors. They couldn't allow the best parts of them to also be in bondage.

We have brothers and sisters of all races and of all colors. We are just as wrong when we hate others who aren't the same color as us. Two wrongs don't equal right. If we chose to stay angry, if we chose not to forgive the mistakes and deeds done to our ancestors, there is someone who holds our wrongs in His hands and the power to forgive those wrongs...He is God. Whether we want to live with anger and un-forgiveness, we're not allowed to and we're wrong. It's the mandate of God to Forgive!

Letting go is hard. It's not for the weak, but the strong. We really have no choice. We can let it go here and now and move forward in our lives and join with our brothers and sisters of all races and colors, or we can answer to God for it later. I don't think Heaven is a place for those filled with hate of the people God Himself created. God made us all! So if we hate any man simply for his complexion, our beef is with God, not the man. I don't think any of us will be standing before a Holy God on judgment day telling Him he made a mistake by creating people different shades and colors.

We'll have to get those things right here in this life before we cross over to our next lives, if we plan on spending them with God in Heaven.

EXCUSES

Excuses are holes in our character. Whenever we open our mouth and disperse them, we shoot holes in our character like an automatic weapon. Excuses come from deficits in our character such as being late, being irresponsible and not being men and women of our word.

We need to be people of Reason rather than people with Excuses. A reason is given before our word or commitment expires. For example, I have an appointment at a certain time and for whatever reason I'm running behind. I look bad by showing up late and giving excuses. I must be responsible before hand and call the person I have the appointment with, apologize for being late well ahead of time and tell them I'm running late and approximately what time I'll arrive. No excuses needed; just an apology, a reason and a call.

A reason is given before your word or commitment expires. An excuse is given afterwards. The difference is one makes you look responsible, the other makes you look irresponsible.

When we make excuses we're telling others not to take us too seriously, that we're not very responsible and we're not very trustworthy or reliable. All of these qualities have to do with our character. A person of sound charter will seldom need a reason to call ahead of time for not making a deadline or being late. But when they do, they'll be responsible and call far enough in advance instead of waiting until it's the normal time for them to show up. They're on their game. They're concerned about their image, their reputation and how others constantly perceive them. These are the reliable employees that you don't have to watch over. Their work ethic causes them to manage their own work. They're a pleasure to have on your team and quite a valuable asset.

Then there are those which show little character. They're late! They don't bother to call ahead of time or at all. As far as they're concerned, you were lucky they showed up at all. When they do show up, instead of feeling guilty, they have an attitude on top of being late. Their irresponsibility is now your problem, affecting your day. They're not concerned with how they look in the eyes of others. They're doing their own thing and will eventually wonder why they've been asked to leave.

Pride is the good we take in being our best. The wrong type of pride is the result of doing things based on our feelings and attitude rather than out of obligation and responsibility.

Let's be people with Reason rather than with Excuses. It will speak volumes of our character.

IN THE VEIN OF PEACE

In life, there are times due to unfortunate incidents which cause us to re-evaluate our current states. Sometimes tragedy is not all bad; especially when tragedy leads us to peace.

God is the author of peace. It's the principle in which He's governed us all to live by. The opposite of peace is chaos. Chaos in the heart of one individual can lead to the destruction of many.

Peace doesn't begin in the world; it begins in the hearts of individuals. It's a thread that must spread throughout the lives of one, of few, of many, to begin to spread throughout the world. Peace must start in one person, in one event, in one activity. One person must embrace its concept, take it to his heart and share it by example, not merely words. Peace as faith; must be backed with action to be true peace. Words are not enough.

Peace is formulated only when pursued. Empty words are vanity. Peace must have substance to work. It must have energy and passion to push it and to bring it forth. It must even have fight within it. Not fight through violence, but through perseverance and sheer determination. Peace without these things is just a word. Words become symbols only when they are backed with substance and great effort.

Peace in this world must start in one heart. It must start by for-giveness and the ability to move past the foolish things we fight over. Grudges must be put down. Harboring bad feelings must be placed aside. A man will never grow with hate, bitterness and resent-ment in his heart. He will remain a small man, seeing no further than his own place in the world, his own ideas, and his own agendas.

No man is bigger or greater than God. No plans are larger than His. No agenda is finer than the one He plans for us all to live by. The plan and agenda of God is one of Peace. That plan must first start in the heart of us as individuals. It's the will of God for all of us. It's His still small voice speaking to each one of us.

To follow God...is to follow after peace.

FORGIVENESS

Forgiveness is more choice than act. One of the hardest things to do in life is to forgive. Forgiveness stems from being hurt along the way of life. Somewhere, someone has caused us harm or pain. Our emotions get involved. Emotions bring with them anger, resent-ment, grudges, which can all lead to hate if not dealt with.

The reason it's so hard to forgive is because of feelings. Feelings are powerful emotions and if not careful, we can live our lives and base our decisions on them. Feelings are products of our senses. Within our bodies and minds we feel pain, hurt, disappointment, bit-terness and embarrassment. We can feel used and mistreated. These can be powerful emotions to let go. We can hold on and cling to these things and not desire to let them go. We want to remember the pain others caused us and use it against them. At times we even want to return the favor of pain through revenge.

Forgiveness is a powerful tool given to us by God. Yes, we may feel that we're right by getting even with the person that wronged us. We may feel justified in our anger and bitterness towards them. But those are all decision of emotions.

God saw fit that one mechanism in life is able to free us. That mechanism is Truth. We may be right to blame, to resent and to return pain for pain to others that mistreat us. They may actually deserve every vicious act we can conjure up in our minds to bestow upon them. No one would blame us. After all, everyone saw what they did to us. The sad fact is, this is how I thought until God imparted truth into my life.

Truth came to me from God revealing that Forgiveness is more of a Choice than an Act. What does that mean? It means that within myself, I will never have the strength to forgive a person that wronged me. I'll hold onto the act. I'll maintain my anger and disgust towards them. I'll allow my relationship to remain fractured with this individual. Forgiveness is a hard thing to do. Don't let anyone tell you otherwise.

But there's a way out! All my life I've thought of forgiveness as an act. It was always something I had to do. It was always a place I would have to go back to. I believed that it was always up to me. I was wrong!

God has shown me that forgiveness is and always has been as simple as a Choice. It's simply a choice I make as an act of the one thing that God can't and will not control in my life…My Will. What this boils down to is, forgiveness is just a Choice for me and an Act for God. I make the Choice. He takes care of the Act of Forgiveness.

Today I live with freedom from anger, resentment, bitterness, regret, disappointment and un-forgiveness. Every day I take the choice to forgive with me throughout my day and use it quite often. People will be people. People will say and do things either without thinking or simply without caring. Yes, I've lived in bondage for the majority of my life as a result of such people and such acts. Not anymore!

God has given me this simple solution to living free. These are the words which led to and keep me on my path to freedom. "God, as an Act of My Will I Choose to Forgive (whomever for whatever). I pray that one day my feelings would catch up to my decision."

With this wisdom from God, it puts forgiveness on a playing field I can handle. The act of forgiving was too difficult for me. I fell short most every time. This way forgiveness is manageable to me. I don't have to do the work. I just have to make the choice.

Chapter 6

Awareness

~~~

The Genius of God is on loan to humanity!

FOOLISH

If you've never been called foolish in your life, then you've never taken great risk, never dared to dream great dreams, never followed a vision given, never created a new invention, never risked your life to save another, never attempted what's never been done before, what's never been seen before, never walked on ground where there was no ground...it was formed beneath your feet only as you walked.

A fool dares to venture into the colossal, while the average man covets the safety of shallow waters. The foolish man sees unlike others. What he sees has been given to him, has been deposited into his mind, his soul, his being. He must pursue it! His life becomes an arrow shooting for one target, one goal. He abandons his own desires to fulfill a higher purpose given to him. He's misunderstood, he's laughed at, he's ridiculed. But what would our lives be like without these fools...like Einstein, Edison, Bordlum, Ford, and Bell.

They were all fools to many, but not to God. They were fulfilling the vision deposited within them by God to enhance our lives. I don't mind being numbered amongst the foolish with man. It's a compliment rather than a rebuke. It means that I have dared to dream, dared to take risks in my life. It means that I've followed the vision deposited in my mind, my spirit and my soul from God. I've become a risk taker numbered amongst the other ones that have taken great risks to enhance the lives of all human beings.

Now I understand what God meant when He said "The foolish to confound the wise." Wise men depend on their intellect. Visionaries, risk takers, follow the dream that's been deposited within them by God. God doesn't make false deposits. If we follow them correctly, they'll pay great dividends.

Any visionary is great whether he fails or succeeds. For at least he has done more than most of us...He has dared to dream!

FIGHT

Today we know little of the true meaning of fight. Yes we know of violence, but violence isn't the true definition of fighting. The weak man resorts to violence only because he can't communicate, so he uses force instead of intelligence.

It takes skill to communicate. It takes time and education to learn these skills. But learn them we must. Our problems can't be solved with our fist and arguing. We must learn to articulate our problems rather than solve them through violence.

Our ancestors knew what it meant to fight. Although they were denied their rights and education, they fought through sheer determination and effort. They used their voices and articulated themselves through intelligence, through ingenuity and through brilliance. These are voices all men must take heed to, because their deeds and accomplishments further the advancement of humanity.

Violence never solves Anything! It still leaves the situation unresolved by forcing the will of the strong over the weak. It's manipulation by force, rather than agreement with intelligence. Violence is never win-win. There's always a looser!

We must learn from our ancestors and teach our children how to fight, but to fight for causes with their voices and communication skills. They must know that waiting on the next guy to come doesn't work...they are the next guy. They must know that the world will not change itself. They must be proactive and responsive and be willing to stand for causes that are just. Then they will know that fight means action, not violence.

It's then they'll be noticed, and given an audience to make a true difference in this world.

STRENGTH

Truth aligns us up to the places we need to be in life. In life we stray from where we need to be, truth repositions us.

One area we've strayed far from the truth in life is the definition of strength. We've moved far from its real meaning. To live correctly and to function in life accurately, we must know the true meaning of things and align ourselves accordingly.

A friend of mine said something very profound to me just the other night. He said "The loudest person in the room is the weakest person in the room!" What he said made a lot of sense. There's a lot of wisdom in the words he spoke.

Today, we've conditioned ourselves to believe that the loudest, most boisterous, confrontational person is the strongest. I know from wisdom God has shared with me, this isn't true!

A lack of control or a lack of self control in our lives is never a sign of strength, but weakness. People who are loud are crying out for attention. People that argue, fight and are confrontational, do so because they lack good communication skills. Bullying another person is never a display of strength. It's weakness crying out for attention and using physical strength to get it.

True strength is in the restraint of power, not the domination of a person or a people. Strength is not always in force. Such is displayed in the arena of sports. Strength in life is displayed in gentleness, meekness, a quiet spirit and sometimes even in silence.

It's the strong person that walks away in silence rather than argues. An argument is strength leaving the body and being exchanged for weakness through the lack of self control and restraint. It exhibits itself through confrontation, through loud noise, the raising of one's voice, and through chaos.

Winning arguments and fighting is never a sign of strength. We've been conditioned to believe a lie. The loudest, most boisterous, the most confrontational and the bully is not the strong one. These are the ones exhibiting weakness through raised voices and hands. True strength avoids such events. True strength uses communication rather than force. True strength is found and displayed in humility, not dominance.

So as of this day, we know the truth about strength. After today if we're argumentative, loud, confrontational and boisterous, we walk right out of wisdom and strength and right into the lack of control of our minds, bodies and mouths.

Now that we know the truth, we must align and realign ourselves accordingly.

HISTORY

History is a stamp in time given to remind us of our places in life. History tells us just how fragile life is. It's a generous reminder that "Hadn't it been for," or "If they wouldn't have," many of our lives wouldn't exists.

History shows us essential events in time which have determined our present and possible futures. Wars and atrocities are displayed before us in panoramic views, in all their tragedy and brutality, to teach us of the mistakes of our past and the sensitivity of our futures.

History's our greatest teacher. Someone once said either we learn from it or we're doomed to repeat it! Wars were won by studying history. Countless lives were saved through strategies studied and employed centuries earlier. History is a magnificent tool. It's a friend that should be studied, utilized daily, and not ignored. It's a tool, just as important as math and science.

Not all of us will be engineers or scientist, but history is for each of us collectively as well as individually. It's an essential part of each of our individual lives. We'll never know who we truly are until we know from where we derived, from whom and from where.

History is our roots that run far deeper than we could ever imagine. In those roots is where we find both the struggles and triumphs of our ancestors. It's in those roots we grasp an unimaginable appreciation, admiration and respect for what each of our ancestors have gone through and survived in times far worse than the ones in which we live, with much less than we could ever imagine.

It's through our history that we focus on the heroes and heroines of our past, and we find that the only words in our vocabulary for them should be words such as "Thank you," and "I honor you" for both your struggles, your survival and even the sacrifices of your lives. Had one of you not survived, if one of you had given up in the face of extreme hardship, cruelty and adversity that was thrust upon you, no one would have blamed you. We still would have admired you just the same.

If that one that gave up, had it been Matriarch or Patriarch... countless of us would not exist today. Our births would have never crossed the lines of time and space through existence.

It's because of you...our ancestors, great grandparents, grandparents and parents that we live. It was your activities, your spirit to survive through crucial times that has given breath in our bodies. It's because you lived...That we breathe. None of you...None of us!

Our history should be embraced, welcomed and honored, the good and the bad, the triumphs and failures, the events which fill us full of pride, as well as the ones that are an embarrassment to us.

Our history marches on. It continues to be written even as these words are written. You and I are someone's history of tomorrow. Let's make them proud!

MEN AND WOMEN OF DESTINY

It was Joseph the "Dreamer" in a similar incident that was promised elevation and prosperity through his dreams in Israel. The plan of God for Joseph was in Egypt, not Israel.

Joseph was spoiled and favored by his father. As a daddy's boy, Joseph would have probably spent his life in Israel. God didn't need Joseph the daddy's boy, He needed Joseph the man of God. Believe me there's a huge difference. The difference is destiny! The lives of others are always affected by a man's destiny!

So how did God Almighty Himself uproot the spoiled boy Joseph and turn him into the man of God with destiny? Through slavery! Once again, slavery was used or allowed by God. God isn't into evil, but being an all seeing, all knowing God, He knows what it takes to get our attentions.

Scene three, we find Joseph plucked out of a pit and sold to travelers headed to Egypt. I'm sure he went kicking and screaming and probably hating his brothers for such a cruel act of betrayal.

Men and Women of Destiny; let me tell you something...The road to Destiny is Never Comfortable. It's paved with potholes, bumps and other factors which make it a very unpleasant experience.

Why does it have to be? Why, if in the end this man or woman is doing something to benefit humanity? After all, Joseph as Governor of Egypt, would end up saving countless lives during the worst famine in Egypt, to include the same brothers that threw him in the pit and sold him into slavery. Why? Because God needs us to be the men and women He needs us to be, not the people we are.

If anyone would've asked Joseph about his experiences of being betrayed by his brothers, sold to an unfamiliar band of people traveling to Egypt, sold as a slave, being thrown in prison for defending the honor of his master's wife, he would have said "It was all worth it!"

As a matter of fact, he spoke words of destiny when he finally revealed his true identity to his brothers coming to buy food in Egypt. He told them what happened to him was the plan of God.

We don't see the fullness of the plans of God while they're in operation and our lives are being acted out in the scene. All's we see is the misery and discomfort we're in. The misery is actually for our benefit, not God's. Our misery is God giving us the pleasure of being used in His plans and what becomes the destiny of mankind through our lives. We don't get to those places being our selfish and stubborn selves. We only arrive to those places by being broken, stripped and emptied of ourselves.

We aren't much good to God in our current conditions. We quit easily at the first sign of trouble, uneasiness or discomfort. God has His ways of making us fit for the Master's use. It's called Pain & Discomfort. Want to be used of God...Expect it!

There are people running around everyday calling themselves "The Anointed" of God. I have news for anyone who believes they're anointed just because they can give an eloquent sermon or sing to make people stand on their feet. God doesn't just had out His anointing. We suffer for it!

The reason being when God uses any of us, Arrogance & Pride won't be found in us. Those things are removed from us by being thrown in the pit, sold into slavery and being wrongly accused as Joseph was.

Sure we won't have the same experiences as Joseph, but God knows what it takes to humble us and to make sure we have Humility & Forgiveness in the end. The litmus test for an anointed man or woman is humility, forgiveness, and the concerns of others not themselves. Don't let anyone fool you! God shares His glory and praise with no man and never will. Many lifting themselves up today are doing it themselves, and not with God.

The work of God is always the focus of God! It's never a specific man or woman having their name in lights and the center or attention. Humility would never stand for that. Being broken wouldn't allow that within a person. Such a person doesn't seek the praise of man. Such a person seeks only the approval of God.

CHARACTER, NOT MONEY IS THE GOAL

The world today pushes us towards being rich. It's what the videos flash in front of our children daily and this becomes their goal.

We turn on the TV on Sunday and now the preacher is preaching financial prosperity. They tell us that God wants us to have wealth. This is what we hear. This is what we believe is God's definition of prosperity and Him blessing us. Yes, wealth has its place in the Bible, in God's plans, but it's not His goal for our lives. God's primary goal for any and all of us...Is Salvation through Jesus Christ! After that His goal for us is Spiritual Maturity and Growth!

After God's initial goal of salvation for us, His next goal for us is Character. Having riches through money only makes us more of what we are. Character turns us into who we need to become. If we're mean and nasty while we're poor, we'll just become more of the same with money. If we're egotistical and selfish, we'll just become more of the same.

With money, these flaws within us are passed off as just being eccentric. It's a lie. Having money should never make up for deficits in our character.

We wrongly play along with these shortcomings in people because they have wealth. It's presented as cool and unique. Such eccentrics will not stand before God. Some of the richest people in this world will be impoverished in the next; if they pass through this one without having Christ in their lives on the other side. All the foolishness and eccentric ways will not amount to a hill of beans when we kneel before God, our Maker.

All the coolness, the playa and the game, all the bling-bling, all the riches, titles and positions we'll leave behind in this world. Those things will burn as fodder and stubble in the Presence of The Almighty.

Yea, we may think we got it going on down here. We may have the praise and the adoration of millions, but on the other side of this life stands the permanent one waiting for us. This life is just practice for the next eternal one. All of our coolness and eccentrics will melt in the presence of God as we look upon Him in All of His Glory and Splendor. We'll know Him as we've been known by Him before our very existence into this realm we call life. For some of us, this will be a short introduction and a one-time meeting with The Almighty. We were the gamers and playas on earth. We will not be when we meet God.

All of the foolishness of our lives will be displayed before our eyes on whatever technology God has that far surpasses our greatest gadget today. It will show us living our lives without the slightest care nor concern for our next one. The scenes will show how God placed writings like this one and people in our paths to warn us of the outcome of our existence if we didn't change our ways and our character.

No, we were too concerned with the ladies, running the game, being the playa, and having all that life could afford us with little or no concern for the spirit man living inside us; the one that would face eternity.

We cared less about this person. This was the real "Us," yet we paid the least attention to him, his needs and his future. That person we see in the mirror everyday was the only one we were concerned about, when it's him or her that will live the least. That person's reflection we see every day, their future and destination has already been determined before we arrived here on Earth. The destination of our pretty, fine and handsome bodies that we pay so much attention to will end up where they came from...Back to the Earth! On our last breath, it's our spirit that will exit. This shell as lovely as it is, will not reach the deciding point of our next destination.

There we'll have no say so in anything. All of our talking would've been done for us while we lived. We will be told where to go and when to go there. We'll have no excuses, as our deeds in life will speak for us where our final places will be spent in eternity.

Knowing this, character should be our pursuit in life. Sure God wants the best for us, but He also knows who would abandon Him if we had millions at our disposal. It's by His grace that some of us aren't rich. God would rather see us poor and make it rich in Heaven than for us to have riches in this life and spend eternity in Hell. Our wealth and good deeds will not account for our ticket into Heaven. God only punches tickets to enter into Heaven when He sees the Blood of Christ upon our lives, as the acceptance of Jesus as our Lord and Savior before we cross over into eternity.

Put all that coolness aside. Leave all of that foolishness and eccentrics behind. Obtain a gentle and kind spirit which is pleasing in the sight of God. Allow God to develop the character He desires in you. So what if you lose some friends in the process. You will be the one to win in the end. When you make that final journey into eternity and stand, or shall I say kneel in the Awesome Presence of God, you'll hear these words, "Well done my good and faithful servant!"

When your friend arrives living his life with coolness, for himself, and the pursuit of riches instead of God, he'll look up in amazement and see God. Even if he'd never recognized him in life, he'll surely recognize him in death. He'll know God as if he'd always know Him and for that period of time, he'll experience all of the goodness of His presence. But just when He begins to desire to spend eternity with the God he never acknowledged on Earth but fully recognizes in Heaven, God will speak these words to him..."Depart from me!"

These are not the words you want to hear coming from the mouth of God. There are no take backs once they're spoken. Off we go into an eternity too horrid to think about, with no decisions, no control... No say so.

We're so engrossed with our present lives that we fail to plan for the more permanent one ahead of us. I don't care how cool my friends or anyone else is. I could care less about their expectations of me to join in their activities. Nothing or no one is worth hearing those dreadful eternal words from God.

Pursue right things in this life. The consequences of not doing so...are Eternal!

GOD ALWAYS LOVES THE LIFE

There's nothing on earth that could ever make God love us any more than He already does. There's nothing we can do to lessen the love He has for us. What we have to know and understand is, God will always love the life. He may not always love our lifestyles.

The love of God is the most consistent of all love. It never changes. It never diminishes. The love of God is unconditional. He loves us no less at our worst and no more at our best.

This unshakeable love doesn't mean God is weak, nor that we just take His immoveable love for granted. It doesn't mean we continue to do wrong knowing that God's love will continue.

Even to the immeasurable love of God, there's a limit. That limit is reached when we continue to tempt the love of God and we stumble into death without taking complete advantage of life. It's the condition of the unwise, to know what's right and continue to walk the tight rope of wrong pushing its limits.

In extreme challenges in our lives, they call this pushing the envelope. It's what we do every day that we live under the love and grace of God without accepting His continuous offer of love. We push the envelope. If we're not careful and continue to push that envelope and tip over into eternity, we'll find the true meaning of... God loves us, but not always our lifestyles.

The love of God will not diminish one iota when we kneel before Him in judgment as he checks to see if we've accepted His offer of love on earth. If we ask God what that offer of continuous love was, He will simply answer...My love offer was My Son Jesus!

He will say to us that what He offered through Jesus was eternal life in exchange for the temporary one we couldn't take our eyes off of. Now we've waited too late to decide as death has brought us over to eternity. Our destinies in eternity are decided on earth while we live.

If we pushed that envelope too often and refused the gift of God while we live, we've made the decision, not God! God's love will remain full for us as it breaks His heart that we must leave Him. At this point, we've tempted the love of God to the point of deciding our own eternity without Him.

He'll love us no less when we left Him with no choice but to speak these words to us...Depart from me, I never knew you! It will break His heart as He speaks them, but we made the choice and left Him with no other options!

Don't continue to tempt God's offer of love. We never know when His next offer will be His last!

Chapter 7

Woman

Every man on earth needs to hear these words...Every woman needs to receive them!

WOMAN

The alphabet was made for you. Words were invented to describe you, but would be found to be inadequate. How can one vessel contain such beauty? You are a marvel! A wonder of nature!

There was no plan nor design ever created to compare to you. You stand alone, set apart and divided by your magnificence. You have no rival, no one to come behind you or after you to neither replace you nor exceed you. Out of all of the fascination in the mind of God...He created you. Chosen from any other or every other design or model, you were the choice of God.

Man was not present when God laid out the design for you. Man had nothing to do with your making. However, he would contribute to your construction only as a compliment, a favor, a gesture of one-ness by God. He would contribute a part of himself without his own knowledge, without his own hand or permission.

The slab of bone and cartilage from man would not be needed for your creation, but was given with great purpose and significance.

The rib was given from part of the man's own body, so that you woman could be a part of him...Equal, separate but one, and unique!

Woman, you may have been created without the knowledge and the permission of man, but man has thanked God for the invasion of his body to create yours. Man may have not been involved in your design, but he has beheld your finished product with great fascination and appreciation!

You are woman...A marvel to behold without rival!

Every one of us has either been culprit or victim in these words!

WE HAVE MISTREATED OUR WOMEN

These are the words God spoke to me tonight while I was on my treadmill...We as men have mistreated our Women!

As with anytime God decides to speak to me, I must stop what I'm doing and respond, "Yes Lord you're servant hears," and begin to take out my iPod and write.

Let me stand for every man in this writing who has every wronged any woman. Let me stand as a symbol to apologize and ask you for your forgiveness.

Let me stand for any man that has seen you for less than who you were created by God to be. Let me admit, as one man standing for all men, that I have lied, stolen, cheated, misled, wronged and abused you woman in every way imaginable. I man, have caused you pain, disappointed you, hurt you, deceived you and robbed you of some of the most precious parts of you.

I man, have been very selfish, self centered and self serving. I have mostly cared only about meeting my own needs and have neglected yours.

I man, have taken you for granted. I have taken your sweetness and giving little or nothing in return. I have taken from you without thanks or appreciation. I have expected from you without replenishing what I've taken.

I man, have treated you less than equal. I denied you the right to vote. I denied you equal pay for equal work. I made you fight for rights that should have been handed to you.

I man, due to my greed have taken you out of our home and placed you in the work force to support my greed for material things and to maintain an appearance to my neighbors and friends.

I man, have neglected to treat you as the feminine flower that you are. I haven't demonstrated my respect for you by opening your door, pulling out your chair for you to be seated and other niceties you deserve. You see, pride crept in and I became ashamed of appearing weak before other men. Well, I was wrong! I now know that the demonstration of love and respect is the highest indication of strength. When I demonstrate my love, my affection and my respect for you, I am only modeling the strength that all men should display. I was wrong if I ever shrunk at the opportunity to demonstrate respect for You in front of Anyone, regardless of who they were and what they thought of me. Momentarily, I forgot that I only answer to two...God and you! I should have cared less what others thought of me. From this day forward I will be better and do better.

I man, was wrong when my eyes wandered when that woman passed in front of us with you by my side. I should have had blinders on and saw only you. I should have held you closer and tighter to reassure you that you are the only woman I will ever need and want.

I man, was wrong when you needed my support, but instead it was more important for me to go to that game, or to hang out with the fellas. I was selfish!

I man, was wrong for all the tears you cried because of me. I was wrong for all of the doubt I created by leaving the house and not telling you where I was going and when I would return. I was wrong for not calling when I was going to be late. I was wrong for coming in late and leaving you home to worry about where I was or what I was doing.

I man, was wrong for taking that which was most precious from you...Your body and your integrity. I told you everything to get it and neglected you afterwards. I was especially wrong if I left you unprotected and you were left to show the evidence of our actions. Out of selfishness, I abandoned you in your greatest hour of need. I left you with the daunting task of raising our child alone, without spending time with the child or meeting my obligations to support them. I man, was wrong for moving on to the next woman and repeating the same mistakes!

I man, admit that I was wrong in these deeds and even worst deeds in my heart and mind. I ask for your forgiveness. I am truly sorry! God has given you as a help to me, and I have hurt you instead.

God would have me to do this so there could be healing within the woman. One hurt in one innocent person can lead to bitterness, anger, rage and hatred. Walls are built to protect a sensitive heart. Standing guard on those walls are the soldiers of anger, bitterness, attitude, apathy, distrust, callousness, and bad dispositions. Ladies you would be justified in each of these actions. You would be if God hadn't designed you and created better for you. Although justified to feel these ways and to act them out, you'll become just as wrong as the one who did them to you if you don't forgive, let it go and move forward.

God's requirement is that you forgive every man for every incident. The forgiveness is not for the man, it's for you. The forgiveness is for your freedom and to remove those toxic issues which escape from your heart and exhibit themselves through anger and resentment through your personality. Although they never should have reached your heart, you must forgive!

God sent this word to free you, to release you from the prison of bad emotions that you've carried for too long. It's time for you to be free. It's time for the Berlin walls to fall which have kept hatred in and kept true love from entering your boarders.

To receive true love you must allow love to flow from a clear heart. Forgiveness cleans the heart, and forces the negative attitudes out and makes room to receive love.

With other words God has given to us, you can now be aware of the signs of game and insincerity in a man. Death to self is the litmus test. If I man, am willing to die to myself for you, then I'm a keeper. If I come to you alive and selfish, kindly ask me to keep moving, as you're no longer in the business of wall building; but being receptive to one man that will build a wall of love around the two of you, where no other will every hurt you again!

Take this first step to your new found freedom by saying this to God...Father as an act of my will, I forgive (name of the man goes here) for (whatever specific act). I pray that one day my feelings would catch up to my decision. The truth is, forgiveness was never up to you. God only wanted you to relinquish your will and your choice to forgive. The act of forgiving is God's department. He only needed your permission which came in the form of your choice and your decision to forgive.

Live free, and now welcome he who is supposed to be in your life, and no more impostors!

A WOMAN'S RESPONSE

I was asked by a friend of mine to share "We Have Mistreated Our Women," with a friend of his. She called me. I read her the writing. Robin and I have become close friends since that day. Here are the words she spoke to me after I shared the writing with her!

WORDS FROM ROBIN

I received, what seemed to be an urgent call, from a male friend of mine. He called to tell me about a friend of his named TJ, who is also an author. My friend told me that although TJ is an author, he doesn't consider himself a writer. TJ considers himself a scribe, for he doesn't write his own thoughts or opinions, but only writes as God instructs.

My friend asked if I would call TJ and allow him to read to me what God had given him regarding man – woman relationships. My friend stated the reading was a man's apology to a woman, and more importantly, an apology that he himself felt, but could not express to me. I thought, "Who is this Cyrano? A stranger to me, one whom my friend had requested to articulate to me words that he himself could not?" And, as women so often do, I did what a man asked of me. I called TJ.

Greetings between TJ and I were given, but no real introduction or small talk were needed. My friend had prepared both of us for this call. However, as TJ began to read a man's apology to a woman, and as I closed my eyes attempting to hear the words my friend's heartfelt but tongue could not speak, I realized how unprepared I really was. I was not prepared for what I heard or for what happen within my heart as I listened to words God had given TJ. Slowly, tenderly, my heart was touched, and in the end, my heart was fully embraced. It was as if God had taken the heart of a woman (my heart) with all its pain, placed it in the chest of a man, and grafted it into a man's own heart. I thought. "At last! At last someone understands the pain I have felt, the pain I have endured, and the pain I still bear - but carry on nonetheless." At last a man has felt the heart of a woman... and understood.

Only God can cause a man to feel the heart of a woman. Only God can cause a man to understand the depth of hurt the heart of a woman can bear at hands of a man. TJ was given such a cause. Chosen and instructed by God, TJ expresses an unusual under-standing of a woman's heart and hurt caused by man. In his writing, he conveys clearly and fully man's need for self-accountability, and communicates it in the form of a well articulated apology.

Men; since this book is written by a man, you will hear a man's voice and it will let you know you are not alone. Moreover, you will hear the voice of all men who are, like you, ready to receive God-given correction and the acceptance of God-given responsibility. In this correction and acceptance, you will find and fulfill the role and purpose for which you were created. Do not be quick to reject the words in this book. For in doing so, you may also, in turn, reject your purpose.

Women; prepare to forgive. Prepare for healing. Prepare to have the protective wall you have built around your heart, brick by pain filled brick, to be torn down. And, prepare to build walls no more.

As our conversation (reading) ended, I told TJ that God will make sure that these words (His words) are placed into the hands of every man and woman who needs them. God will send these words exactly where they need to go. My example: When TJ and I spoke by phone, we had not yet met. That night, TJ spoke the words God had given him through a phone and into the heart of a woman, and a complete stranger. Healing began and hope sprung new.

If you are reading this, it is not an accident. It's on purpose; His purpose...and yours.

THE NOT SO SILENT CRY

We are the cause of who you are. We are the cause of where you are. The pendulum must now begin to swing in the opposite direction. God has heard your cry! Your cry may have been hidden in your room, but it has not been hidden from the concern and the ears of God.

Over time, women have become the way they are because of the way we have treated them as men. We have hurt them, used them, misled them and abandoned them. Our actions have been the cause of women going into the construction field. It's a field she doesn't belong and never should have gone. But she has, for her own protection and survival.

The construction field the woman has gone into is the one of building walls. She's become a master wall builder when God never designed her to be. She stands behind these walls and even hides behind them. She hides her true nature and her true self. What's seen in society isn't always the woman God designed. That woman's been hidden behind the walls she's built from mostly the hurt and distrust of a man.

A woman can never be the woman God intended and designed her to be hidden behind walls. Walls protect, but they also don't allow the right person in. Every day, walls cause women to miss out in ways that God's attempting to bless her.

Here are a few examples of the walls a woman's built in her life. A woman may build a wall for her own protection, but the wall will always show through her personality. Walls show through the character and personality of a woman in such ways as distrust, confrontational, mean, nasty, hard, callous, distant, demanding, domineering, independent, and selfish; just to name a few. Looking at this list, none of these qualities have anything to do with who God wants a woman to be. But unfortunately, it's how many have become.

It's the not so silent cry of a woman! She may look nice on the outside, but she's screaming on the inside. She screams because she's out of her place, the place she was designed to be in. She screams because she's not in her proper role as only God has created her to fill. She screams because she's seen for less than who God made her to be; and devalued.

She regrets trusting men, who only leave her after he promised her the world. She screams because she trusted such a man and lowered her defenses to give him the most precious thing she owns...her body. Now the man has moved on, and she's left with children to raise alone without his help. A woman was never intended to raise a child alone. So she screams inside because she's been placed in an awkward and uncomfortable position she was never meant to be in.

A woman cries, because now her personality has been altered due to pain and disappointment. She looks back and wonders who she's become and how she got there. The once innocent, sweet flower has been plucked instead of being watered, pampered, admired for its beauty, cherished and cared for.

Just as the man has to take responsibility for his part in how women have become, a woman has to take responsibility for knowing who she is in God's eyes before she can be seen right in the eyes of man. Once she knows who she is in the sight of God and realizes that she was designed for so much better, then she'll not allow Anyone to be the cause of her personality and character changes. Only God will take that role in her life.

This doesn't mean that she's arrogant or haughty. This means she knows who she is with humility and grace, and now protects herself with the wisdom and discernment of God, rather than walls which show through her personality as negativity and unpleasant mannerisms.

She must let go of the pain and forgive to be free. A woman can no longer allow society, a man, and her unsaved girlfriends to dictate who she is. She must allow God alone to show her and tell her who she is and the purpose for which He made her.

It's then she'll shed all of those unwelcome traits that have come with the construction of the walls she's built. These walls must come down! Because behind the wall is a delicate and beautiful flower which will never be seen by the world and One man. These walls must be traded for wisdom and discernment from God.

The world, society and the devil wants you to stay in the construction field and to keep building negative walls around you. Satan knows that as long as you stand behind them, you'll never fulfill your purpose from God. You won't be the woman with a gentle and humble spirit which is pleasing in the sight of God. Instead, you'll be tough, defiant, distant and cold. Such qualities God never intended you to have as a woman He designed and created.

No longer let a man define you. No longer let society dictate who you are. To be right for the One man God is preparing you for, you must move away from the world and it's foolish ways of thinking and concepts of how a woman should be and embrace the destiny that God's placed within you.

God made you beautiful, strong but gentle. No longer fall short of your destiny. Use the wisdom of God to discern if a man's right for you. Please know, God will not send you a bad man to convert him or change him. Ladies, that's not your responsibility, nor is it your charge. God is the only one capable of changing any of us. Such a man will only bring you down and you'll end up blaming God for something He had nothing to do with.

A man God sends will already be responsible when God sends him. No, he won't be perfect nor without faults. Such a man will be more concerned with your needs than his own; because such a man understands the precious gift from God you are as a woman to him.

With this man, you can put your cement and steel away which you use to build your walls with. You'll trade them in for your carpentry tools. With them, a man may build you a house, but you'll be the one to make it a home.

DESTROY THEM EARLY

Never in my life have I learned so much. I've become a student of the words God shares with me. His words bring insights and enlightenment, discoveries and new observations. It's as if scales are removed from my eyes and now I see vividly and clearly.

Today was one of those days for me. God spoke a word to me and in all my years of life, I've never saw what He spoke to me. I was amazed, enlightened and made wiser all at the same time. What a precious gift from God!

These are the words God spoke to me today. He said "The plan of Satan is to destroy the woman early!" He showed me what He meant by this. The strategy of Satan is the same as it was in the Garden of Eden...Destroy God's creation man! Once one of the most beautiful of all angels, pride took over and He lost his place before God. God created man to praise and worship Him now. The mission of Satan became to disrupt this intimate relationship God had with man.

In the garden, he used the closest thing to man...Woman! Adam knew better than to eat of the forbidden fruit. Satan didn't even tempt him directly to eat of it because Adam knew better. So he would use his cunning ways to appeal to the woman through her sensitive and emotional nature. He convinced her! She would now convince the man to eat through her emotions, her appearance, her body, her perfume or whatever else she used to cause Adam to do something he knew God told him not to do. Probably for the first time in his life, He sided with his wife instead of with God. Mankind has been paying the penalty ever since!

Satan's goal was complete...Destroy the man through the woman! This one act of disobedience produced the fall of mankind. It threw life and the earth out of balance. It caused death and life was stolen from humanity. But God had a backup plan. He's never caught off guard.

In that same garden stood the Tree of Life. He was always there waiting for His fruit to be eaten for eternal life. He was Jesus! He would one day take the form, shape and appearance of the man He would buy back and redeem unto God.

Today the strategy of Satan is the same...Destroy the man through the woman! Just his methods are different. There is one thing each of us must know before we can be effective in life and in the world. That's our purpose! We must know why we're here. We must know our roles to be successful. We must know them to be obedient and to fulfill our destinies upon this earth.

Today Satan's strategy is to destroy the woman early! The purpose of the woman God created was to help the man fulfill his destiny through the family. If the woman never gets to the man or if she is destroyed and extremely damaged before she gets there, then neither of them fulfills their destiny given by God. This is the strategy of Satan, to get to the woman before she can become effective for the man, and the man can become effective for God.

God is all about purpose and destiny, whatever He does will be about purpose and destiny. One of the ways Satan gets us distracted and off track is to focus on ourselves rather than our destinies. If we only see ourselves, we only benefit ourselves. A man or woman of destiny can affect countless lives.

Here's Satan's plan! Get the woman while she's young. Bring a young man into her life that she's attracted to. Have him tell her a bunch of lies about how much he cares for her, how she's the only one for him and get her to lower her defenses. One time won't hurt he says! She gives in believing that he cares, and one time won't hurt anything. It was a lie in every way! The truth is, all it took was one time to produce a child. The truth is, now he's gone and wants nothing to do with her. Now she's pregnant and all alone.

Get her pregnant. Get her to have not one child, but several. Get to her before she realizes her purpose. Get her to give up on her dreams, ambitions and goals. Take her focus off of those things and have her to believe she'll never accomplish any of them. With each child, have her give up more on her dreams and settle for a life she never intended to have.

Get her to waste her potential. It's the strategy Satan uses. Now her self esteem is low. Instead of moving forward with wisdom and awareness, she can't get the one mistake out of her mind, the one she gave her heart and body to, and the one that only used and abandoned her. Instead of rising up, getting help and getting her life back on track, she settles. Another one comes along and assumes she's an easy target because she has a child already.

He comes, full of game and lies. She lowers her guard again. Another child is born. Another man's gone. If she doesn't get help and guidance, she'll fall into a rut of self pity and shame and wrongly believe she's no good for anyone. That's a lie that Satan wants her to believe. He wants her to believe her life is wasted and to sink even lower.

Some other things happen. Because she's been tricked, deceived and lied to, this once sweet young lady has become hurt, confused and disoriented. Where has her life gone? What about her dreams? What about her plans for a good husband and marriage? Through the years, she's now grown into a woman. But due to hurt, pain, deceit and un-forgiveness, her heart which was once sweet and sensitive, has now been covered over with stone. Her heart is guarded. She's built a wall of stone around it to defend and protect it. Instead of the once sweet personality, now bitterness, anger and attitude have replaced a quiet gentle spirit which was once pleasing in the sight of God.

Satan believes he's won! He believes he's destroyed the woman and her potential. He believes he's destroyed the man she was intended to help fulfill his God given purpose on this earth. He wins only if we allow him to win. Damage has been done, but there's always hope in God. God can take our greatest tragedies and turn them into triumphs. But we must allow Him to.

What can happen? God can send a man to such a woman with the intent to love and care for her. Maybe her self esteem is low and she's afraid of being hurt again. She may push such a man away who was only sent to love her. Death is always the answer! Is a man willing to die to himself for the sake of a woman and the relationship? This is the test! This doesn't mean that he takes you shopping and buys you everything you demand. That's not reality. What is closer to reality is if a man demonstrates through kindness, care and concern that he will care for you, provide for you, love you with understanding and be committed to you.

Don't be tricked by roses and jewelry, seek the substantial, lasting qualities of a man. So what if he's handsome! What good is that if he uses his looks to cheat on you with every woman around! Of course we have to be attracted to the person we have a relationship with, but the best qualities are the ones on the inside. Beauty can always captivate us, but it can also blind and mislead us.

The best case scenario is to take this wisdom given to us by God and know the tricks and traps of Satan. Pregnancy is his biggest trap to destroy young lives before they get started. Don't be wasted potential! Don't fall for the deceit that can lead you down a dark path to bitterness, anger, resentment and a bad attitude. God has so much more in store for your life than broken dreams and a broken heart.

But you must be wise early in your life to become the flower God planted you to be. You must be quick to see and fast to learn the barrage of request from young men coming to you. You must not fall for the "Just one time won't hurt," line. It will hurt! You'll pay for it for a lifetime! He'll be long gone with someone else while you're left all alone with a child you will rise on your own.

God has an excellent plan and purpose for your life. He can also have a man that will care for you and love you as He intended. But don't let your life be ruined with hurt, pain and bitterness by the time he finds you. Be alert and know your destiny lies with One man. Not a perfect man, but a mature, responsible, reliable dependable man who will treat you like a lady and respect your qualities as a woman.

Please be aware that Satan will attempt to destroy your life early, before you even reach all the vast potential God has placed within you. Don't fall for it! Be who God created you to be and join your destiny with a man who is looking to fulfill the destiny given to Him by God.

THE BEAUTY OF YOUR PERSON

God made a flower from a rib. He made a garden from cartilage. The most beautiful flower on earth is not in plant form...It's in the form of a Woman!

God made you beautiful, feminine and soft to touch and to hold. He made you gentle and nurturing. He made you a welcoming presence to every home. He made you the jewel of one man you call husband. You are the most beautiful creation of God. Your are woman!

Within God's creation of beauty upon the earth, you have many to compare to, but none to exceed you. Even the seven wonders of the earth do not measure to the beauty God placed within you. Nothing on earth will ever exceed the beauty you behold.

Being such a wonder, it would be a shame for you woman to withhold and to hide the beauty God Himself gave to you. Unfortunately, there've been culprits that have caused you to do just this. The culprits are I man, and society. We've made you into something you were never intended to be.

God gave a woman tremendous beauty, femininity, gentleness and care. Look what's happened! Because you woman have been tricked, deceived and constantly lied to, your sweetness and sensitivity has been exchanged with harshness and caution.

You were not designed to be on a constant state of alert, looking, analyzing and deciphering what man is bringing to you is truth or lies. Remember, God designed you for one man, not many. One good man with a heart from God alleviates these games. It's unfortunate that a man's approach to you today is with the intention of game.

Love is not a game. Your feelings are not a competition and a sport to be given to the winner who deceives you. There is nothing "Game" about love. A game is a sport with one winner and one looser! Love is not a sport. It's a union designed by God to have two winners, no losers.

God made you woman different, unique and with no equal. Look at what's happened. A woman's had to defend herself from lies, foolishness and deceit. She believed she had to be tough to survive. I man, have left you stranded plenty of times. I haven't always entered your garden with the intentions to only care for, tend to, nourish and love you as God instructed.

Instead, I man, was a wolf in sheep's clothing and my real intentions were to fleece you, not to maintain your garden. I man, was a wolf disguised as a shepherd. I've robbed you of your precious plants and flowers. In defense, you've had to appear tough and guarded. Your femininity has suffered as a result of this.

One of the most beautiful parts of a woman and what makes you so unique is your femininity. It's something only you possess. It's what makes you exceed all of God's other magnificent creations. But unfortunately, you have abandoned some of this uniqueness and put on the image of toughness. God made you gentle, strong and soft. Being tough is a quality God gave to man, not woman.

Women today even make excuses for being feminine which is totally wrong. It's who God created you to be...Feminine and Beautiful. Today instead of a woman referring to herself as a feminine flower, she labels herself as a "Girly girl!" A woman shouldn't have to make excuses for being who God created her to be. The problem will lead you back to I man, and society. I man, for causing you to become something God never designed you to be and society for making you believe it was alright to become less of who you are.

There is a remedy to this problem. It's called Wisdom and Awareness. A woman must first realize who she is and what she has is precious. She must also be aware of and not naive about the fact, that she has in her possession something every man wants and will sink to no lows to get it. She must use wisdom to release herself from the temptations and ways of society to fall for the "Gamer," the bad guy or the one she's attracted to but knows his intentions are wrong. So many women fall into this trap of falling for the wrong man. He will only reap havoc in your life and leave you in the wake of his selfishness; alone, abandoned and un-cared for.

There is a man that God sends to a woman praying for a good man. But he comes without the game. He's a nice, kind, gentle man with pure intentions. He would make a good husband and care for the woman all of his life. He would love her and only her. He would sacrifice himself for her and take the role of leader in his home as guided by God. He would pray with his wife, pray for her, and serve his marriage. He would work. He would first have a place of his own and not live with his mom. He would establish his own household first and then send for his bride.

Not working, staying at home and playing video games while a woman works, would never be an option for him. He would never belittle a woman like that. He would never send her out into the workforce while he stayed home and did nothing. Such thoughts would never enter his mind.

He wouldn't come to deceive, but would come as a shepherd and be a shepherd. His role would be one of protection, not to harm, fleece, rob, mane or steal from you. He would be a man of his word and of his commitment. He would honor God; respect his marriage and his wife. He would lie on Isaac's altar before the wedding as a living sacrifice without squirming, without complaining, nor trying to free himself from the ropes. He would die to himself for the sake of his marriage and his wife. He wouldn't achieve perfection in this, but maturity.

Maturity is what a man possesses and a player doesn't. It makes all the difference in the world. It will make the difference between having one man...Or suffering from many!

But what usually happens when God sends such a man into the life of a woman? She's not used to him. Something's wrong! He's too good to be true! She can't believe after all she prayed, this could be the one. He's not the normal guy. He doesn't come with all the bells and whistles of deceit. He simply comes as himself, as God sent him to be...No tricks, no game! He's a gentleman and wants to open your door, pull out your chair and hold your hand in public. He sees beyond your external beauty and sex is not his intentions, but getting to know the woman that you are on the inside is. Sure he's attracted to your beauty, but he cares about you the person.

He doesn't come full of empty and broken promises. He doesn't have a wife across town that he's planning on leaving for you. He's responsible, and if he has any children, he cares for them and is an intimate part of their lives. He doesn't run from his responsibilities, but accepts them as a man. He's serious about serving God. He's not perfect, but he always tries to become a better servant of God, man, husband, father and contributor to society.

What should end up as a productive life for the two of them, ends with the woman pushing this man away. Because he's nice, she sees him as weak. She's gotten used to the rough one, the thuggish ones. She's been deceived to believe this is who she needs and who can make her happy. If she wants game and irresponsibility, she's going to get it. She may get what her eyes wanted, but she'll quickly find out that she got the wolf instead of the shepherd. He's now got what he wanted and now he's gone to the next farm. The good man, the one sent by God is gone and may never return.

The woman goes from one bad relationship to the next because in today's times its worst than ever. Women are more beautiful than any other time on earth. This just makes for more game and more deceit for an irresponsible man to conquer, deceive and abandon.

A woman must be wise. If she's praying for a good man, then she must open her eyes and heart to receive him when he's sent to her by God. No, he may not be what she expects. No, he may not be the gamer that you see on TV. God isn't into foolishness and doesn't waste lives and feelings. No man will ever be perfect of course, but God will send a man of maturity, with good values, respect and the desire to serve both God and the woman he marries.

Why is it that the virtuous woman in Proverbs is considered a wonderful example of a woman and wife, but if a man contains the qualities he's supposed to from God, he's considered weak? That's a lie that Satan and society has caused a woman to believe so she would end up hurt, bruised, injured and bitter, so she wouldn't fulfill her purpose on this earth given by God...To help One godly man complete his assignment given to the family. If the enemy can keep a woman trapped and focused on the wrong kind of man, she will never fulfill her purpose on this earth.

Ladies be wise. Use wisdom and no longer walk in deceit. Don't hold back an ounce of the gift of your femininity. Allow the right man to come to you and release all of the beauty God Himself has designed you to display. For you are indeed...God's most beautiful Creation!

LET A MAN BE A GENTLEMAN AND A WOMAN A LADY

You can tell a society not by the times in which they live but by the respect we demonstrate towards others.

Today's society is skewed. The pendulum has swung in the wrong direction so that wrong appears as right and right appears as wrong. Strength appears as weakness and weakness appears as strength. It's a backwards time we live in. Our ancestors would be furious at our foolishness and blatant disrespect for ourselves and others.

A man who demonstrates respect for a woman is not old fashioned, he's just respectful. He's a gentleman, a man worthy of respect. Today he's considered weak!

There are still men that believe in opening a door for a lady. There are still men who rise out of respect for a lady when she approaches the table. There's men that still pulls her chair out for her and gently pushes it forward after she's seated. These are honorable men who demonstrate respect and deserve respect as they're setting the proper example for all men.

Such a man is not always appreciated in these times. When a respectful man is not seen as a value nor appreciated, the society in which he lives is in trouble. This has never been more evident than in today's times.

Many women today want the thug, the rough man with little manners and very little respect towards her. Somehow she finds the bad boy fascinating. He's irresponsible, unreliable, and untrustworthy and the list continues, yet it's him she's drawn to. It's deceit! It's a lie! Its believing something bad for you is right. If you really think about it and analyze it, it's foolish!

How can anything bad be good for you? It's the same deceit Lucifer used in the garden to fool Eve...Believe what's wrong is right for you. That lie, through deceit caused the fall of mankind. Through our woman believing and falling for the same deceit through Satan today, our society is perishing.

It's still the same lie through the same devil. It's just wrapped in today's times. Satan's strategy is still the same as it was in the garden, attack the woman to destroy the man or mankind.

Unfortunately, women fall for this deceit everyday and are left as single parents in the wake of it. God ordained that children would be born out of marriage and have both mother and father to raise them. Satan's plan is the opposite of whatever God's plan is. His plan is to destroy society by destroying the family. He wins every time a woman falls for the bad boy instead of the responsible and mature one. The results are devastating. Women are raising children alone. The father is no where around as an authority figure for the children to respect and listen to. It's not the way God intended His society to be run. It's the opposite of order. It's chaos!

We must be wiser. We must do better. The pendulum must begin to swing in the direction of right instead of declining towards wrong. Wrong is never right, nor will ever be. Bad is not good, no matter what slang we use in the times we live in. If we start off with bad we'll normally get worst. We've got to stop falling for the lies of the devil. We must change our way of thinking towards truth and awareness which in turn will cause us to make better decisions.

We must stop only thinking of ourselves and consider the children we bring into this chaos without their permission. They arrive here to life in confusion from our bad decisions. It's not fair to them.

We're responsible for contributing to society with good decisions. Ladies, let a gentleman find you. Let him respect you as you deserve to be respected. Let him treat you as the lady that you are. Let him admire and adore you. When he comes, don't take him for granted, nor misinterpret his strength for weakness. He's actually the strong one. His strength is demonstrated through his care, concern and admiration for you. His strength is demonstrated through his reliability, dependability and responsibility towards you.

Open your eyes and your heart to accept his strength and no longer believe that the bad boy will ever be good for you or good to you. Yes, you may find him attractive, but sin itself is very attractive! Attraction fades and becomes unattractive when the real person shows himself. Being left, robbed and used is not attractive.

Ask God to give you the wisdom to be attracted towards he who is right for you. It may require you to place your feelings aside for a moment for you to see the truth. Feelings are the main things that mislead us as they're tied to our flesh. This is not a flesh decision. It's a life decision. You can't afford to have your flesh involved in it. This decision must come from your heart through the wisdom of God.

SERVE THE PURPOSE WHEN YOU CAN'T SERVE THE MAN!

Women, when you find it hard to serve the man...Serve The Purpose! You will not always find that the man you married is in tune and on track with God and his purpose. These will be difficult times for you no doubt, as your destiny is tied with his. This is why we must be clear of a person's potential before we cross the bonds of marriage. But if you happen to accept Christ on the other side of marriage and your husband has yet to come to the Lord...Serve the Purpose of Marriage if you can't Serve the Man!

In marriage as a woman, your destiny is connected with that man you married. Marriage is unlike dating or going together as we can't just jump up and say "I'm breaking up with you!" That's not what we signed up for at the wedding when we made those vows to God, not to the preacher.

The Bible tells us that the heart of the man can be won over by the attitude of the wife if he is an unbeliever. This is when a woman is at her strongest. God is not talking about strength as in putting the man down, belittling him or making him feel less than a man. Regardless of what today's society says, that not strength...That's weakness! That's the path of least resistance. It takes no strength to tear a person down. True strength is in building and uplifting. A wrecking ball can do plenty of damage to a home, but it takes loving hands to build one.

It's a difficult role you have as a woman. I see that as God reveals this to me through this writing. I've seen it in person. It's difficult to serve God knowing your role as a wife, accepting that role, and not having a husband who accepts his. Don't let anyone tell you that it's not difficult. Your future is tied to this man! You go as he goes! The family goes as you go together. That's a difficult position to be placed in. That's why it's essential to know that a man has died before the wedding. He can die afterwards maybe, but you'll pay the price while he lives.

What does a woman do when she didn't know this word before she got married? What can she do to live her life according to God and honor Him in her marriage to a man whose not being who he's suppose to be and walking in the role God has called him to walk in? She can serve the purpose of her marriage until she can serve her husband in the marriage.

There's something God shared with me that will help every woman out there in this position who has attempted to use her own methods to change the situation. Remember these words God spoke to me, "A man can be guided, but not pushed!" Ladies, now you know why your strategy didn't work when you tried to manipulate him; to force him and demand him to change. It doesn't work!

The worst thing you can do to a man is to make him fell like he's less than a man. A man should have within him the ability and the desire to lead his family. He may have been made to feel inadequate by your words and attitude towards him, so he became what you said he was.

If a man constantly hears he's no good, he doesn't know what he's doing and he's a poor leader, then your words have given you what you spoke to him. God gave us the Bible for a reason, to learn from it. One of the greatest examples of a woman's strength in the Bible is the virtuous woman. Her husband praised her. He was successful in his career as he sat amongst the elders. She was mostly responsible for his success through her support and the encouragement of her husband.

Proverbs 31 tell us in these verses what this woman did to win the trust, respect and love of her husband. "10 Who can find a virtuous woman? for her price is far above rubies. 11 The heart of her husband doth safely trust in her, so that he shall have no need of spoil. 12 She will do him good and not evil all the days of her life. 26 She openeth her mouth with wisdom; and in her tongue is the law of kindness. 28 Her children arise up, and call her blessed; her husband also, and he praiseth her. 29 Many daughters have done virtuously, but thou excellest them all. 30 Favour is deceitful, and beauty is vain: but a woman that feareth the LORD, she shall be praised. 31 Give her of the fruit of her hands; and let her own works praise her in the gates."

No it's not easy being in a marriage where a man isn't fulfilling his role as ordained by God. This can make for a very difficult marriage. But God didn't leave us ignorant of answers to any situations we face in life. We can always find the answers in His word. God gave the example of the virtuous woman for this reason. The answer lied within her attitude and the treatment of her husband.

Who's to say her husband wasn't being a bum at first. Who's to say that her marriage wasn't any good and she felt no different than you feel about your marriage right now! Maybe she listened to the words God spoke to her, and decided to serve her marriage until she could serve her husband. Maybe this is how she became The Virtuous Woman we speak about, admire and reference her example thousands of years later. No one ever became great by doing something easy!

Being great will always cost us. Doing anything worthwhile to affect the lives of others will cost us too. Fussing, fighting, screaming, hollering and demanding a man to change won't do it.

He may change for a moment to get you to keep quiet, but his heart hasn't changed. His ears just wanted silence. A true change will only come from his heart. A man's heart can't be changed with force... But only with love!

Pushing and pulling won't do it. His heart must be guided. If he isn't the man he needs to be, ask him to be what you need him to be. If he doesn't know his role, humble yourself and explain what you need from him. God didn't give him mind reading powers, so let's get that out of the way first. What God did give him was a proud heart or an ego with the desire to lead when he's allowed to.

If the man is taken out of his role, he has no role until you as his wife gives it back to him. If you've taken it from him out of desperation, turn it back over to him and work with him until he walks in it as he should before God. After all, God designed you to help him.

But remember, belittling him or putting him down may be tempting, but it's wrong and will only work against you in destroying your own home. Take the strong route that builds up and encourages your husband to succeed. Just as your negative words tore him down and he became what you spoke of him, so will your words of encouragement build him up to become the success you speak him to be.

Who knows, that may be exactly how the virtuous woman's husband in the Bible was so successful and praised her so easily... Because she spoke him into being the man she needed him to be!

HEAD BY DEFAULT

There's something that destroys more marriages and families than anything. It's disorder in the family, or specifically the disorder in the leadership in the family.

God is a god of order, purpose and structure. He designed the family. He established the order for it. He also models the correct order in the family through the example of the Trinity. Within the Trinity is perfect order. It's the example we should follow for the order of our marriages, households and families.

The Trinity is made up of God in three persons. The miracle of God is three, yet One. There are not three God's, but One God in three persons...The Trinity. The Trinity consists of God the Father, Jesus the Son and The Holy Spirit. The three operate in perfect order. How do they do this? They do it with one simple word...Submission!

Submission is a word we hate today, especially women. But I'm here to tell you that you as a woman should have hated it, because those that told you what it was lied to you to get you to do what they wanted you to do!

First of all, Submission is one of the strongest acts in the world and in life. It's not being weak as man has wrongly portrayed it to be. It's not just laying down and being a doormat either. That was wrong of man to do that to woman, to misuse the word submission to get what he wanted from you. That's called manipulation! It's wrong!

The essence of Submission is...Strength Given for a purpose greater than yourself. There is absolutely nothing weak about submission! It's strength demonstrated in its greatest form. It consists of being vulnerable, exposed, unselfishness, giving all and love itself. These are not characteristics of the weak, but the strong and mature. These are the difference makers in the world. These are the obedient of God. These are His Kingdom builders on this earth.

Within the Trinity exists the perfect order for us to follow for our marriages. God is the Head and both Jesus and The Holy Spirit submit themselves completely to Him. Now that we know the true meaning of submission, we can see it clearly through the example of Jesus. There was never a time that Jesus did His own thing. He totally submitted to the will of God even unto an innocent, horrible death. Even when it was difficult, He continued to follow the will of God for His life. He was completely sold out to God! He did what God required of Him for the good of humanity.

God's will, that each of us must submit to, is no different than the will of God for Jesus. The magnitude was different of course, but to impact lives as its primary mission is the same. In our marriages, it's the will of God that we submit our lives to each other.

Here's something else man has neglected to tell women... Submission is required by the man if not more than the woman! The scriptures doesn't really come out and tell man this in the same words as clearly as it did with the woman. God had to make this plain with the woman because of the order He established in the marriage and in the home. For the man, it was just suppose to be known that he must submit his life unto his wife.

As a matter of fact, he was required to submit his life even unto death for her. He was commanded to love his wife as Christ loved the Church and died for her. Now that's submission required in its highest form!

Now that we can see truth about order and true submission in the family, these power struggles in our marriages must stop. God made it clear that the man is to be the head of the family. Now we know that he must submit his will to both God and unto his wife in the administration of his duties as the head of his family.

The wife was created to help the man fulfill his purpose from God for the family. The wife wasn't designed to be the head of the marriage, but to function as the Administrator of the family. As we can already see, she has the gift to direct what goes on in the family. God has given her the ability to juggle many things to assist with the management of the family. This is her role. She was never designed to be the head of the family.

Let's fast forward in time to today. A woman's had to assume the role of head of the household by Default. She's had to assume this role she was never created for due to the fault of man. Either he's absent from the home, doesn't know his role, or refuses to take responsibility to walk in it.

To function out of the order of God is disorder. Disorder causes both chaos and confusion. It destroys our marriages and families every day. It must stop!

We must be wiser in the choices we make. We must think of the consequences down the road and how they'll affect not only us, but our children. The reason God instructs us not to sin is because of the consequences we suffer from them later.

Look at all of our children being born outside of marriage today. Look at all of the women being left to raise these children alone. Absent man doesn't take care of his responsibilities, nor has he placed his union with this woman in the bonds of marriage before he laid down with her. It was obvious that he didn't even have the consideration to protect her in the act and left her with the possibility of disease and child. How can this be love?

Woman and child are left alone while the man has moved on to the next victim. It's a vicious cycle that must stop. Fathering without being a dad is weakness on a man's part. Left alone, the woman has now been placed in the awkward position to head the family. It's a role she wasn't created to be placed in. Her role from God was to help, not head!

We as men must stop this cycle of being fathers and not dads. We must know and understand that marriage is the place to produce children. Within the marriage we must die to self, we must die to our own agendas, and we must die to the fact that our wives are not our slaves and servants, but equal partners in God's purpose for our families on this earth.

We must use wisdom to know that submission is required on our part as men first before it is ever required by our wives. We must first submit ourselves and have her best interest in mind to even marry a woman. We must convince her that she'll be safe, protected and cared for in the marriage. But most of all, we must convince her that she'll be loved! This is strength and the power of submission in action. It's the requirement of God for the man.

Just as God requires the man to lay down his life for his wife, she must lay down hers also but in a different way. She's not required to physically die for her husband, but she's required to die. She must die to her own agenda and selfishness just as the man. The woman has power, strength and wisdom. She brings these qualities into the marriage. Submission is having great strength and abilities but laying them down and using them for a common good; for the whole or for the one.

In the marriage, the woman must use her abilities for the good of the marriage and not to get what she wants. This is manipulation on her part if she uses her abilities for this. She wins; they win, only by combining their abilities and strengths and using them for the destiny of the marriage and family.

Marriage consists of roles. Each must know their roles and function and remain in them. Today we see the confusion and destruction in marriage by not operating in our places. Our children are being raised by single parents. God designed them to be raised with the influence of both mother and father. Let's use this wisdom God's shared with us to renew our marriages, our future marriages and our lives in accordance with the order of God instead of the chaos we've experienced that will only continue to ruin what God intended to be good for us.

LET HER KNOW

Let her know she's a winner. Remind her that out of all the millions of women in the world, you chose her! Tell her how much you appreciate her, and how attracted you are to her. Thank God for creating her!

Sometimes walk behind her and soak it all in! Watch her as she sleeps and thank God for each breath she takes. Admire her differences and bring them to her attention. She wasn't built or assembled; she was gently placed together by the loving hands and the infinite wisdom of God. She was made with grace and beauty. Marvel in her femininity. She's a woman! She's a beauty to behold!

Draw near to her and embrace her with love and kindness. Let her be all the world to you. Let her be your light and the glow that shines within you. Give her your time and attention. Tell her she's the one for you, the only one. Don't place her life on hold by anyone or anything. Let no one or nothing distract you from her love.

Let no game, no friend, no golf match, no fight, no child, no nothing come before her. Forsake all for her when she needs you. Make her fit into every part of your life, instead of finding ways to exclude her. Let the fellas know she's number one in your life. If she can't come, then you can't come! Let her know, let your family know, let your friends know that you respect her, that she's your life partner, that you're One, standing united against the world if necessary!

Give her your best. Cleave to her and keep her close to your heart. Keep her name on your mind and on your lips. Be a man to her and not her child. Don't expect her to treat you like a child, to chase after you like a child, or to pick up after you like a child. Be a man!

Give her someone to respect and to release all of her inhibitions and fears in. Fertilize her garden with trust, reliability, dependability and responsibility. Give her a reason to release all of her fears, her doubts, and the pains and disappointments of her past within you, with a new fertile ground of love and trust you'll provide for her.

Let her take a leap into your arms knowing that you'll catch her. Never let her doubt your commitment to her, for her and with her. Tell her often how you cherish her and adore her. Remind her that she's all the woman you will ever need, want and desire.

Be a man with strength who expresses his love for her instead of one that wrongly believes that it's a sign of weakness for a man to be expressive and candid with his affections. We as men have believed that lie from Satan for far too long. We've wasted countless days and hours being tough, non expressive, and withholding our feelings instead of expressing them. These are moments we can't get back. They are lost in time forever!

Let your lady know she's a lady, not a man! Treat her as such. Don't be rough with her; be gentle. Speak words of kindness to her. Monitor your tone, your words and your delivery of them.

Men, your woman is dependent on you to provide her with an environment in which she can release all of herself to you without fear or regret. She's dependent on you to fertilize her garden with love, with peace and with awareness that she's unique, different and very special. She's dependent on your trust to make her feel alive and to release the woman God has created her to be.

Her trust in you will release her from despondency with you. You must prove to her that other than God, she retains first place in your life. You must demonstrate to her that no friend, no game, no toy or material object will ever compare to the affection you have in your heart for her. It's not enough to believe this, you must desire it, you must want it, but most of all, you must display it. Not for a day, for a week, for an occurrence or just to get what you want. You must display this daily without ceasing. You must be committed to adopt it as part of your character towards her and part of your lifestyle. It must be a permanent change in your heart.

Men, you're the leaders in your homes. You can't wait for change; you must be the device which brings it. You're the initiator. You're responsible for making the first move. Your wife is a responder. She responds to the environment you provide for her. She can do no more. She's a product of your love and your intentions to do her good or harm.

We all want the woman in Proverbs 31. Yet, we were all ignorant to the secrets of how this man allowed his wife to become that woman until now. Today the truth, the wisdom and the revelation of God has met us where we stand. After today we are without excuse. After today we're accountable to God and our wives to create an environment for her garden to grow, for the flowers of her femininity to flourish, for the petals of her love to grow with trust in us as husbands and men. We're no longer without wisdom or excuse as men.

The Word of God has come to us today for enlightenment, for direction and purpose. Take what you've heard, adopt it into your lives. Erase the old tapes of lies Satan rewinds over and over in your mind. Replace them with the wisdom of God that came to you today. Allow them to come alive within every part of your being. Watch the changes in the life of your wife, your children and your home.

Be the light of the world God intended you to be to a world, to marriages and hurting families trapped and suspended in darkness. Share what you've learned with every man you meet. Let them see the change in you and wonder what your secret is. Make them desire what you've received. Let them ask, "What must I do to be changed?"

Be a conduit which brings the electricity of light into countless homes. Let them blow out their old fashioned candles of living in their old ways without knowing these truths from God. Help them come into the new understanding of the light of God for their marriages, for their homes, for their children and for their entire lives. For He's The Light of the World; The Great Illuminator. He's our Beacon to Heaven and to living life abundantly on this earth.

WHEN OUR PASSION IS AN EXTENSION OF OUR LOVE RATHER THAN JUST AN EXCUSE FOR MEETING OUR PHYSICAL DESIRES, WE'VE CROSSED OVER FROM THE

BONDS OF EARTHLY LOVE TO THE REALM OF PURE LOVE GIVEN ONLY BY GOD.

Make The Change!

KILL THE MANS DREAMS, KILL THE MAN

I've never heard this truth spoken so plain and clear before. These were the words of the Bishop where I was blessed to speak. This man knows about dreams. He marched with Dr. King for the dreams and freedoms for all people. In his many years of ministry I'm sure he's seen many marriages destroyed by the profound words God spoke through him. "Kill the man's dreams, kill the man!

It's what we have as men. It's what's been given to us a leaders in our homes. It's what God provides us with to direct the lives of the family we've been given stewardship over. If we're not allowed to dream and lead our families, we will shrivel up, clam up, shut up and die. We may not physically die, but when we die to our dreams, we die to the life within us. We have little to focus on. We have little to push our lives. We live life without a compass or direction. We're lost!

A man must dream! It's one of his gifts from God to direct his family. Today men are stripped of their dreams. Many times the woman works and can make more money than her man. She can wrongly use this as a weapon instead of the blessing for the family that it is. She can wrongly use this against her man to degrade and humiliate him. She can destroy him. A couple is one. What is done to one, is done to the other. So many couples fail to realize this. What you do to the other, you're doing to yourself!

Women must learn that after they marry, they get the man they speak with their words. Ladies, your husband is a product of your words. He's a product of the words you speak to him, the manner and the tone in which you speak those words to him, and the contents in your words.

Some women have mastered the art of disabling their men with their words. Her initial goal was not to be controlled by him, so she worked on him by withholding affection, sex and concern for him. He knew she was the only place he could get these needs met. So when he went to her and was rejected, he stood a little smaller in his eyes and in hers. Soon, instead of standing tall, he began to grovel before her, begging her to assist him with his needs. She then had him where she wanted him, weak and not in control.

Now she'd use her words on him, tearing him down further, aiming her arrows directly at his manhood...Delivering the final blow! He was no longer capable of leading the family, so she stepped in and took over. Now he sits off in his easy chair alone with no say so in his own house.

His woman, in her attempts to not be controlled, has broken him. She's damaged his spirit. She got what she spoke! Her words were made manifest right before her. Sadly, how many times does this go on in marriages...Far too often!

A man is like a building. Either a woman builds him up or tears him down. She's left with what her words made him to be. Then she blames him for becoming what he is. She loses respect for him. She manages the house without his input. He's a shell of a man, not a man. He's been stripped of who God created him to be by the woman he was given.

For the family to succeed, he must be restored. She must restore him with her words and her affections, and not just sit around and wait for God to do it. God's not coming down here and whispering sweet nothings in his ear, speaking to him in a soft and gentle tone which draws him instead of making him not wanting to come home. It's his woman's place to restore him. It was her that broke him!

Never has any woman been given permission by God to break her man. You will never hear such foolishness from God! Man is God's man. He was God's first human being on earth. It was he that walked with God first, whom God gave dominion over all the earth and named every animal we see today. It was he God gave the command to not eat of the fruit. It was he that God held accountable no matter what action his wife took.

The woman was given to man by God to assist him and to enhance his life, not to destroy it! She wasn't given to the man to drive a wedge between he and his Maker. She wasn't given for him to grovel, and follow after her as a child begging to get his needs met. He was meant to stand tall as the man God created. He was created with so much interest, and given so much responsibility from God his maker.

God didn't make Adam a boy, he was a man. He was fully grown and aware of who he was and who he was created to be. Why would God create someone to come and disrupt what He designed man to do and be on this earth? He wouldn't and He hasn't! Women that walk in these ways have adopted their own agendas and have abandoned God's. There's no excuse for this. There's no reason that God will accept from you.

Man was His first created being, not his last. He was given the orders for the direction of the family. He was given the dream. He was given the vision. He was given the assignment. He will one day stand before God and give an account in how he led and directed his family. His wife will stand and give an account on how she supported him with his mission from God.

God will know whether she erected a mighty edifice or created a shack. He will know just by the way her husband stands before Him. If he stands bent over and dejected, she built a shack. It he stands tall and proud, she built herself a palace.

Ladies, the choice is in your hands!

Chapter 8

Marriage & Relationships God's Way

Once we cross over into the bonds of marriage, we are no longer in our own territory...But God's! It's why it's called Holy Matrimony!

NO FUNERAL AT THE WEDDING

Marriage is God's domain. He makes the rules and they're unchangeable. We're not allowed to modify, adjust, tweak or remove the laws according to our own selfish desires and pride. Flowing with the times won't cut it in God's sight either. We're to be a peculiar people; set apart and to stand out for the world. How can they respect our witness if they're the ones leading us? That's backwards. We're to be the light on a hill to the world that can't be hid. That light is our lives, it's our examples we display only as we follow God; not man, not society and not ourselves!

The problem with every marriage that ever ended up in the divorce court could be summed up in these words...There was no Funeral at the Wedding! At a proper marriage, there are the marriage vows which take place. But prior to these vows, a funeral must take place!

The wedding vows are obvious. The funeral... Not so obvious! I found out today only as God spoke these words to me. It's revelation knowledge that I couldn't come up with in a million years. God only speaks truth. What He spoke to me today was truth.

We fail in our marriages and every marriage that fails, fails for the same reason...No funeral! In every funeral, someone has died. In the marriage funeral, both bride and groom, husband and wife agree to die right up there on the altar. What a fitting place to die... The Place of Sacrifice.

Man and wife must agree to die to selfishness, self centeredness, pride, chaos, confusion, conflict; power struggles and to die to the obedience to the headship that God has established for the marriage and family. They agree to die to un-forgiveness, revenge, bitterness and unsolved anger. Marital death is hard. It takes tremendous strength, vulnerability and sacrifice.

Marriage isn't for the weak, the selfish, easily startled, unreliable, irresponsible and quitters. Those people might as well continue to date and not jump into ruining someone else's life and dragging the poor children into their mess.

Marriage is for those who believe in a lifetime commitment. Yes marriage is hard, but you push through. God designed marriage with only two doors...The Door of Entrance and Death! Death was the only exit door designed in marriage. It was the hardness of the heart of man and woman that forced The Door of Divorce. God never created that door. He allowed it due to our rebellious hearts.

A dead man feels no pain is what they always used to say. Those of us that have died to ourselves in marriage and in life don't care about how we look to others. We don't care what Joe and Sally are doing in their marriages. We don't care what society said was OK.

We forgive, we sacrifice, we apologize, we humble ourselves both husband and wife to benefit the marriage. We fall in alignment with God's laws and leadership for our marriages. We kick pride out of our marriage. We put foolishness behind us. We take the fight off of us and take the fight to the enemy's camp where we become warriors for God, taking back and tearing down the strongholds and the lies we've fallen for.

We become strong men and women, husbands and wives, being a beaming light for other marriages and helping to deliver them out of darkness, deceit and the subtle tricks of the enemy. We become God's kingdom builders on this earth. We're a light and an example to our children on how to have a successful marriage, so they never enter the vicious cycle of parenting children alone without the needed influence of both father and mother.

To get here, it will cost us something. It will cost us our lives. Not our physical lives, but our sacrificial lives. For a successful marriage, we must all follow the example of Isaac. When his father laid him on the altar as the sacrifice required by God, he didn't complain or try to free himself from the ropes. He laid there as a willing sacrifice unto God. He accepted the will of God for his life even if it meant the death of him. God is looking for such willing vessels in marriages.

After today, I know these are God's requirements. But we kick, we squirm, we're full of pride and selfishness. We're unlike Isaac, but need to be. To enter marriage, we must first be willing to lay ourselves on Isaac's altar and let God raise us from death as new creations, men and women in the covenant of Holy Matrimony. Then we must be mighty warriors, keenly aware of our adversary and taking the battle into his camp and destroying his works on this earth.

Let there be...No Marriage Without A Funeral!

THE MIRACLE OF ONENESS

It's a miracle that we overlook every day. It's a miracle that we even fail to acknowledge. Our parents and grandparents understood this concept. When a woman married, she became Mrs. So and So; whatever his last name was. Her identity was now blended with her husband's.

Fast forward to today's times, a woman will keep her own name in marriage or hyphenate it to maintain her own identity. God said that the two become One! This is what God said in the beginning of time, He still means it today! His words, rules and laws are absolute and apply to all generations and times. It's not the times in which we live that should govern our decisions. God's laws don't change and are not subject to the times in which we live. God's laws supersede the times.

Either we're in alignment with God's laws or out of order by making up our own rules in which to live by. There's only one law and that's God's Laws. Either we live within them or sin outside of them. There's no in between.

We have neither right nor authority to change the Laws of God. Just because others are doing it, just because it's fashionable, just because it's an indication of the times in which we live, it's still wrong! God says we're One! One in all ways, not the ways we pick and choose to be.

If it were a physical transition on our marriage day and we were joined together as flesh and bones, then it would be more obvious. In the physical realm it would look like Siamese twins joined together, but not exactly. It would be even closer than that. This is a spiritual union, like no other on earth. There are no two addresses. There are no two mailboxes. It's the home, the oneness of Mr. & Mrs. Jones. It not Smith-Jones, it's not Smith. When we join together in God's Holy Matrimony...We play by His rules!

WE'VE BEEN TRICKED!

We've been tricked! The oldest, slickest plan of the Devil is to keep the focus of the couple on themselves and they never move forward. It's the old strategy of fight amongst yourselves and it takes the focus off the real enemy. If he can keep the couple focused on a power struggle in the marriage, then he's won.

What happens is, the couple enters into pride. Pride is the same trick Lucifer used in the garden with Eve. In our case, the couple fights. They fight over who's in control, over who's the leader. Instead of them both submitting to the headship established by God, they establish their own. They fight, they argue, they're constantly mad at each other, wondering why they got married in the first place.

The Devil's winning, as he's caused the couple to take their focus off of him and keep it on themselves. When you're fighting in your own camp, you never take the fight to the enemy's camp. An effective enemy is a blind enemy; one you never see, or one who hides behind another and makes you think they're the enemy.

It's the oldest trick in the book and we fall for it every day. The divorce courts are full of it. People so much in love just months ago, now can't stand each other. Another marriage, another family, the lives of more children ruined due to our blindness that led to our selfishness.

How we disappoint God! Really, our vows were made to Him, not the preacher, not the Justice of the Peace, and not the hundreds of guests at the wedding. It was a covenant between God and the couple. It wasn't an agreement to date or to go steady. It was a life covenant eternal in the Heavens. It was an immoveable, unbreakable bond in which God added the finishing touches and defied the Laws of Physics and made two people One.

THE LADY LION, THE TIGRESS

God made you both, beautiful, powerful and strong. Within you is the capability to take down a full grown man and devour him without the slightest of problems. Yes, you are beautiful, capable, powerful and strong; lady lion and tigress, but you are also a lady to one.

You must know and use wisdom when to be the tigress and when to be the lady whom only one must freely enter and protect you. You must know when to retract those powerful and magnificent claws, capable of ripping skin. You must know when not to show those teeth which hold the capacity to take the mighty ox down at the jugular. You must know when to expose your belly to be rubbed, caressed, pampered and played with.

Yes, you are the mighty lioness, the magnificent tigress...but first, God has made you the lady, with long flowing hair and smooth caressing skin. You were made to be entered by one man; who is the mighty lion, to protect and honor you. You weren't meant to always be on guard, on alert, and on notice. Even with your skills and your power, you were meant to be protected and honored by One.

He is the Lion! He must not always see your teeth and claws. He must see your belly, telling him it's safe to enter your environment; that he is both welcomed and wanted. He must know it's safe to enter. He must know he comes to protect what only God has given him.

He must know that you look upon him for comfort, strength, protection, care and love. He must see the glow in your eyes and not always the snarl on your lips that tells him not to enter or bother.

Just as you are dependent on him to fulfill his role as head, as protector, as provider; he is dependent on you to allow him to be.

Show your lion your belly and watch him be the lion in all he was created to be. Continue to show him your fangs and claws; he will see you as another lion...Not the lioness God made you to be!

DEATH IN A MARRIAGE

Death is a journey we must make alone. One death required per person. I can't die for you and vice versa. We must each take our journey into the abyss. We each must die to self!

If one alone takes the journey, the marriage will be unbalanced or unequally yoked. This will be a deficit relationship at best. One will make all the sacrifices. One will require the other to make them. One will give and one will take. There'll be an unbalance of love and an unequal distribution of it.

The giver will feel used, frustrated and worn out. Eventually they'll feel they've nothing left to give. The one who refused to die, has drained and exhausted them with their lack of support, lack of giving and contributions.

The dead one appears weak to the live one. They give and they give while the one alive continues to take them for granted. In truth, the dead one is strong and exhibits this strength through their obedience to God. The live one demonstrates their weakness through the lack of discipline, support, selfishness and disobedience.

It's a 100% to 50% relationship. It's a relationship of deficit with only one receiving the benefit. It will produce misery, chaos, dysfunction and frustration until Both die to self. Unfortunately, usually by this time, the exhausted one is walking towards the divorce court!

Dating has no rules, no guidelines, and no laws. Marriage does! Only the serious and the brave should enter. Once we cross over into the bonds of Holy Matrimony, we've entered into the realm of God. The requirements are a whole new set of rules. God alone sets them. We're not allowed to change them no matter who we are, what our titles are, what our income is, nor how important we think we are. Agreeing to marriage, is agreeing to follow God's parameters.

Marriage is also not the arena for believing that we'll change the other person once we get married. The only person God cares about us changing is ourselves. As a matter of fact, what destroys so many marriages is ignorance. Believe it or not, one of God's goals in marriage is to change us. In marriage, we've placed ourselves within the confined walls of God and seeking His direction for our new life together as one.

None of us come into the marriage perfect, without any baggage and hurts that haven't been dealt with. Besides that, we come with our own issues God was working on within us prior to the marriage. God finally has us in a place where we're not supposed to run, but remain only until death separates us. He knows there's junk within us, so He begins to work on us to remove it. He hates to see us weighted down with unnecessary baggage. His goal for us is liberty and freedom.

His work begins. He puts His finger on an issue in our lives. Maybe it's anger, maybe it's a bad attitude, maybe it's negativity, or maybe its rebellion. God wants it! We don't need it. It only hinders us and eventually reveals itself through our personalities and relationships. It's got to go! We've held on to it for years. Like pulling teeth, the process begins.

Situations come about in our lives that require us to act out in these areas. Maybe our new spouse hasn't seen this side of us. It's ugly! They're shocked! If we haven't died to self, we're still in the blame game. Instead of looking within ourselves, we lash out and blame our spouse for our shortcomings. Words like, "I was never like this until after we got married!" "You bring out these things in me!" "You bring out the worst in me!" The blame game is the coward's way out.

Maturity dictates that we accept responsibility for our own actions and recognize our need for change. We even blame the devil for our actions. No, he's not the culprit; it's our sinful nature, which God is attempting to clean up in our lives.

In marriage, expect it! Those without wisdom will blame God for giving them the wrong person. They'll retract their statement indicating they weren't the one God brought into their lives. God is simply cleaning house! If you want to blame someone, blame God! It's Him that's at work.

Sometimes we look no further than the person in front of us, instead of the person in the mirror; and panic. "What a mistake I made marrying this person," we say! It was no mistake, it's a process.

God's goal for the couple is maturity. Maturity comes through test and eventually passing those tests and moving forward. Maturity comes from being aware of what God is doing in our lives and accepting responsibility for who we are, our shortcomings, and our desperate need for change.

Death is a road we must walk alone. Dying to self and our flesh is a personal journey we take with God to join together successfully as husband and wife. When God says it's time to get on that road, don't resist, don't fight it, don't blame...Just Go!

It will be the most rewarding journey of your life! It will lead you on the path to freedom, peace and maturity.

THE PURPOSE OF GOD THROUGH WOMAN

For any of us to know our purpose we must go to the One who created us, and see why He created us. Within the purpose of that creation lies the answers to our existence. When we walk according to the plans from The Manufacturer, we live and operate efficiently. When we go against The Manufacture's plan, we operate in dysfunction. There are only two ways anyone or anything can operate... Functionally or Dysfunctional.

For a woman to know her true purpose, she must go to the Source and discover why she was created. This she we will find in Genesis 2:18, "And the LORD God said, It is not good that the man should be alone; I will make him an help meet for him. 20 And Adam gave names to all cattle, and to the fowl of the air, and to every beast of the field; but for Adam there was not found an help meet for him. 21 And the LORD God caused a deep sleep to fall upon Adam, and he slept: and he took one of his ribs, and closed up the flesh instead thereof; 22 And the rib, which the LORD God had taken from man, made he a woman, and brought her unto the man. 23 And Adam said, This is now bone of my bones, and flesh of my flesh: she shall be called Woman, because she was taken out of Man. 24 Therefore shall a man leave his father and his mother, and shall cleave unto his wife: and they shall be one flesh."

The purpose of the woman is defined by God Himself in these words. Now that a woman knows her purpose, she will choose whether she will walk in obedience or disobedience; whether to function correctly or dysfunctional in it. God sets the parameters. He makes the rules and the laws in which we live by. He's The Manufacturer of us all. He or she that was created should never ask "Why did you create me like this or for this;" but "Show me Lord how to properly walk in the ways and purpose for which you created me." Such a person displays wisdom; those that take the other route of wrestling with why, will continually have problems.

Here's an example of this from the words of Solomon in Proverbs 4," A virtuous woman is a crown to her husband: but she that maketh ashamed is as rottenness in his bones."

Going back to Genesis, we see that God decided it wasn't good for the man He created to be alone in this world. So He created him a helper. What did the man need help with? God had already given the man instructions on what his role was on the earth. He would need help with his purpose and he needed companionship. This would come in the form and shape of the woman.

The woman, God fashioned from the rib of the man, was created to help him, not to hinder him. She was created to support him, not to tear him down. She was created to fight for him, not to fight with and against him. When we walk in the roles God assigns us and created us for, we honor Him. When we walk in our own ways we dishonor Him, and serve our own selfish nature.

Really nothing's changed in Satan's strategy since God created the first woman. His strategy is to destroy the purpose of man through the woman. He used this same strategy in the garden with Eve to destroy the intimacy Adam shared with God. Don't think for one moment that Satan enjoys the fellowship God has with man after he was thrown out of Heaven. He hates it! He'll use anyone or anything to destroy and disrupt it. He'll use the closest thing to man to do this...His relationship with his wife. A woman must know this!

A woman must be aware that Satan will use her against her husband to prevent him from doing the work God's assigned him to do. She must be wise. She must be aware. She must be keen and always watching. She must be above what other women in today's times are doing. She must stand above what her single girlfriends are doing. She must block out the poor examples she see's on TV.

To be a woman of destiny, she must not fall into the temptation to tear down her husband, but build him up. She must look to support the mission of God through her husband. Proverbs 14:1 says "Every wise woman buildeth her house: but the foolish plucketh it down with her hands."

There should be a casket or a cot to serve as a symbol of the death requirement at each wedding. This would serve as a reminder to the newlyweds of the requirement of God for their marriage; that for a successful marriage each of them must die. The couple is normally so focused on the wedding, they forget about the requirements of the marriage.

Not only should the couple symbolically be placed in the casket, but also, each one must place some things in there with them. They should place the thoughts and desires of old boyfriends and girlfriends in there. They must place the hurts, the pains and disappointments of past relationships in there. They must place bitterness and un- forgiveness towards others that have hurt them in there. They must be willing to see only the person in front of them, not the ghosts of past relationships.

The difference between knowledge and wisdom is this. Knowledge is having the information we need to make sound decisions in our lives. Wisdom is knowledge applied to our lives in any given situation. One is having the information but not necessarily using it. One uses the information.

Here's a test of wisdom each of us should apply before we say "I do" and enter into marriage. We must ask that potential spouse these two crucial questions. Are you willing to die to yourself before you enter into this marriage? And are you willing to stay dead? The problem is, there are plenty of opossums entering into marriage. These are the ones that play dead but are still very much alive. They say all the right things, act all the right ways and put on a good face at the wedding. But when the marriage starts...It's on!

Out of nowhere comes a totally different character and personality. We don't recognize this person as that same person we fell in love with. The mask and the gloves have come off. The niceness fades, the neatness goes to the wayside and you get the real, raw person. They weren't really dead, but pretending.

Some don't even pretend. They're shocked to find that after the marriage and the fun of the honeymoons over, the marriage is at home waiting on them. Some get overwhelmed at the responsibilities, commitment and sacrifice it requires. If death hasn't occurred, selfishness creeps in. Self preservation, not self sacrifice takes place, and it rolls downhill from there.

Marriage is hard work! The couple must not be ignorant to this truth before they decide to get married. Sacrifice is hard to a living individual. The very word sacrifice means giving something away you may not get in return. That's work for those of us who are alive. It's not so hard for those of us who are dead to self.

If only One agrees to die in the marriage, there's no marriage. Marriage requires two on one accord. If one refuses or is unwilling to die, we must know this up front. Many of us find ourselves so in love and can't live without them and proceed with the marriage anyway. We're just asking for trouble! We've open the door to a lopsided relationship. In the Bible it's called being unequally yoked.

A yoke is that wooden harness that goes around the neck of two oxen to make them work together. Imagine having one oxen and one mule in a yoke. This is a physical illustration of a spiritual truth. This is what we'll get in a marriage with only one death. If both refuse to die and proceed with the marriage, then you get two mules in a yoke.

The question of death must be asked prior to the wedding, not after! We must not be ignorant to the warning signs during the engagement period. Dying to self doesn't mean that one person takes advantage of the other. Sacrifice is not making the other person demonstrate they'll give us what we want to prove our love. Coercing a person into giving us what we want is called manipulation. Manipulation stems from selfishness.

A dead person doesn't use the person they love. The essence of love is sacrifice. Without sacrifice, there's no love!

Now that we know different, now that we've been given knowledge from God to save us from foolishness and heartache, it's up to us to use wisdom and apply the information we've learned. The Bible says "My people perish for lack of knowledge." This day, we've not lacked the knowledge we need to succeed in our marriages.

MARRIAGE IS LIKE A BABY

Sometimes God speaks His words to me directly through my mouth. They're spoken right in the middle of my conversation with someone. Such wisdom and insight I know didn't proceed from my mind...But the Mouth of God!

Today as I spoke to my cousin on the phone, these words proceeded out of my mouth..."Marriage is like a baby!" She said "I never looked at it like that before!" Neither had I!

There's a huge misconception in marriage; that a marriage will take care of itself. Marriage is actually like a new born child. It's no different actually. It needs constant feeding, attention, nourishment and changing.

If a baby isn't fed, it cries. If it doesn't get attention, it's neglected. If its diaper doesn't get changed, it stinks. If it received no attention, no effort, no love, no nourishment...It would die!

We've been ignorant to this fact. We've just entered into marriage and expected it to take care of itself. We've expected it to do the work for us. We sign up for it; then we sit! It's no different than a man getting married and now he just sits in his easy chair all day. Something and someone is getting neglected when we just sits.

There's a difference between sitting and resting. Sitting with the intent to neglect work is being lazy. Resting is with reason. Even a child needs to rest. So does a marriage. It sometimes needs to rest from its responsibilities, let its hair down and have some fun. It needs a vacation too. It needs for the couple to have fun together and get away to a different environment for a change.

Marriage is a child that will require your constant attention. As with any child, it grows and matures. But the marriage child will always remain a child of some sort. Even until death separates the two, the marriage must remain a child. There's never a point that it must become a grown, self sufficient adult. It was never designed to be. It will always require the couple's full attention.

Marriages fail every day. They die of starvation. They're not fed, watered or nourished. When there's fallout, bitterness and anger, these become the dirty diapers that if not changed with the diapers of forgiveness, huggies and pampers, we'll wear those stinky diapers everywhere we go. We'll wear them to work, to church and the stench of them will be exposed through our attitudes towards others.

They'll show up on our jobs through our anger and bad attitudes due to our problems at home. They'll show up in our lack of productivity at work as we'll lack focus and concentration, because our hearts are torn apart from the separation and lack of peace in our marriages. A bridge of forgiveness must be built to rejoin and restore us to our proper places.

Marriage is work; hard work. We only deceive ourselves if we enter it believing otherwise. It's hard and equal work for two, not just one. Both must contribute. Both must sacrifice. Both must die to self. Both must realize that although they are two grown individuals, they'll always have a baby on their hands that needs their constant care, love and attention.

They must know that no matter how many children they bring into this world, they'll always be left with one when the others have grown and left home. It's the Baby of Marriage, their first and permanent child. It will never leave home!

ROLE REVERSAL

If we would just sit down for a moment and seriously think about some things, we'd realize how we've been deceived in life. When God takes the blinders off our eyes we're able to see the subtle traps and tricks of Satan. The sad part is, without this revelation from God, we just live our lives in disorder and believe it's the right way to live.

It's not! Satan's plan is to kill, steal and destroy. Stealth is his greatest weapon. If he can't be seen, he can't be blamed! If he's not to blame, then we blame others instead of taking responsibility for our own actions and the part we play in things.

Satan has a bull's eye on the family! If he can destroy the family; society is ruined. Families make up society. Destroy the structure, weaken the foundation of the family, and watch it crumble is his plan. The sad thing is, we fall for his tricks everyday!

Never in society has there been such confusion and disarray in the family. Roles are reversed or non- existent. Never before have we strayed so far away from our places and purpose. Marriages are a mess and the poor innocent children we produce suffer the most. Not to mention the damage done to children born outside of marriage without both parents. That's another issue entirely.

The best and most successful team in any sport is a team full of role players, a team where every individual knows their role and purpose on the team and sticks to it. Michael Jordan was my favorite basketball player. He won six championships! Not with superstars, but with players who accepted their specific roles on the team. If your job was to play defense, that's what you did. You weren't out there shooting 3-pointers. For the success of the team, you sacrifice your individual desires.

This doesn't happen in marriages today. Both husband and wife want to be the stars of the team. Both want the ball. Both want to take the last shot. They want to argue over whose team it is like Kobe and Shaq did. Who cares! You're members of the same team. You win or lose together!

One of Satan's strategies is to have the couple take the focus off of the purpose of the marriage and place it on each other as individuals. Here comes the conflict! Now, one person's needs outweighs the other. Now, one feels slighted and less important. The battle begins!

Instead of the couple standing together, the relationship is splintered due to selfishness. Instead of one goal for the marriage and family, now there are individual goals. "I want my own spending money!" "I make my own money!" "As a matter of fact, I make more money than you"! " I deserve the right to spend it as I please!" These are just a few of the unfortunate words spoken in the battle.

God made a husband and wife One, regardless of who makes what! You're a team! What one has benefits the other. There's no room for individual stars and free agency in the marriage. You're on this team for life. They'll be no midseason trade. You won't be up for Free Agency in the off season! There's no off season in marriage. Only our selfishness seeks to be traded to a new team through divorce. Selfishness is the root cause of every divorce.

So many times a man is confused in his own home. He no longer knows his role because the woman has taken it. God instructed him to be the leader, the captain of his team. But the wife has her own opinion about this instead of God's. Instead of her standing side by side in support of her husband, she stands toe to toe with him. It's Ali and Frazier all over again!

A couple who faces each other in conflict will never move forward. Logic dictates that in order for two people to move forward, they must be placed side by side, not toe to toe. Facing toe to toe, you won't go anywhere and you'll blame the face you see in front of you for your lack of movement.

A woman doesn't want to hear this, but God requires you to humble yourself in your marriage. If you want your husband to be the man God created him to be, walking in the role He created him to be in, then you must relinquish any desire you have to control him. You must relinquish your desire to humiliate him and not allow him to walk in his God given role. You'll never have peace; you'll never have order in your household without humility. A man can't walk in his role until you relinquish your position as pseudo head of the family.

Satan's job is to keep conflict and turmoil stirred up in the marriage. It's our job to recognize this, to be wise and to take the battle to him instead of on ourselves as a couple. He wants us to fight over whose team it is and who's in charge. Again, it's a toe to toe posture instead of one in which we both humble ourselves and stand united side by side.

In today's society, a woman can make more money than her husband. It's not uncommon at all. This woman must be who she is at work, but when she comes home; she not the executive, she's the wife. Not that her role at home is lessened in any way, but she falls under the headship of God in her home. This can be a huge issue in marriage when it shouldn't. The couple must know their roles in the marriage at home are not reflective of their careers at work.

The career can be brought home and placed into the marriage. Most of us work in a secular world where the rules are completely opposite to the laws of God. We must be wise to know and understand that our secular positions don't translate into our marital roles. If a woman is a judge on her job, she's a wife at home. If the man is a sanitation engineer on his job, he's head of his household at home.

We must face it; this is the way of God for our marriages. Yet we've been tricked, blinded and deceived to believe otherwise. We've lived so close to the edge of the world that we've adopted their ways, mannerisms and bad habits.

Roles or shall I say, proper roles, are the foundation of a good marriage. Without them, our marriages are built with straw and are easily burned and consumed with the fiery darts of Satan. Being a role player is a position of strength, not weakness. A role player takes their position for the success and benefit of the team. They sacrifice self satisfaction and personal accolades for winning a championship.

Maybe we were free agents and superstars when we were in the dating realm, but when we signed our contracts for the marriage team, we became role players. Our contract was to perform a specific role. We signed up as a team member who would be depended upon to bring our unique skills for the betterment of the team. Our Coach told us before we signed the contract that the only way we succeeded, was as the team succeeded.

Our Coach warned us that the opposition would attempt to distract us and tempt us to walk outside of our roles. But this is why He gave us these instructions, so we'd be prepared when the temptation came. Our Coach is a winner and has never lost a game nor a battle. He knows what He's talking about. He has a 100% success rate for those who follow His instructions.

Our Coach not only prepares us for the game, He prepares us for battle. Our opposition must be found and exposed! He must be defeated! With the success of our marriages and families are how we defeat him. He wins through divorce and broken families. It's a battle we can't afford to let him win through deceit and unaware-ness of who he is and what his strategy is to defeat us. Through the wisdom of God we're not ignorant of his devices and can take the battle into his camp instead of our homes.

Our mission is clear from our Coach...Destroy the works of the enemy! We can only do this as role players on a team...Not indi-vidual superstars with our own agendas.

Chapter 9

We Must Do Better

Prejudice & Hatred are learned traits...They can be unlearned with Education & Awareness!

I'M BLACK...BUT MY FOCUS IS ON GOD!

Yes, I'm a Black man and I'm proud to be. When God predestined my life and my position in the world, He placed me in the perfect place geographically and racially.

I couldn't be prouder of my Black heritage. No other people in this country have started so low but have risen so high. It's a monumental accomplishment if you look back and see what a race of people have become through the most horrible conditions and treatment. Our people survived the worst unimaginable cruelties, lived to tell about it and flourished upon the same land and ground. It boggles my mind to even imagine some of the hardships they came through yet survived. Those same hardships and turmoil became a life of freedoms and privileges to countless Blacks today.

Our people were extremely intelligent and many were self educated because they understood that education was the only tool that would place them on a level playing field with the rest of society. Education wasn't a free gift and opportunity to blacks. The laws forbid it, yet that wouldn't stop them from receiving it. Knowledge is key. Wisdom is outstanding. Our people knew this and exceeded the lofty standards they placed upon themselves even through the bonds of slavery. They wouldn't be denied their God given right to knowledge.

No one could be more proud of our people than I, but I don't see things from a Black perspective, I see them from God's perspective. It's a wonderful thing to celebrate our history, our tremendous and amazing accomplishments here in America, but we're not the only people here. When we only look at ourselves, we place a barrier of exclusion between others.

Yes we must celebrate who we are, where we came from and the pride of our heritage, but the requirement of God is to live peaceably with All people! We must see all things in our individual lives as well as our collective lives as a race from the eyes of God, not the viewpoint of man.

Man doesn't always forgive. He doesn't always let go of as God requires. Man can be full pride, hatred and remorse. He can always look to the deeds of his past and carry them into his present life. They will show through his personality as un-forgiveness and bitterness. A man isn't truly free with such characteristics in his life. He may attempt to let go and join his proper place in life, but this place requires both of his hands to be empty. He can't join his God ordained place in life while bitterness and hatred occupies one of his hands. He needs both hands for grasping and clutching his neighbors on equal sides of him.

I'm sorry to say, God doesn't see thing from just a Black perspective nor any other race of people. God see's them from the perspective of humanity. He sees them as any father would with children with different characteristics and personalities...As His Children.

God has many children as He is Father of us all. We are only brothers and sisters of different shades and varieties. This was the choice of God, not man. Variety is the paint brush of God. It's He that chose our shades and our pigmentation; and when He looks upon us, He see's splendor and variety through His handiwork. It was man who took a look at the varying shades of a people and saw disgust when he should have seen the variety and handiwork of God.

Anyone who has a problem with the shade of man has a problem with God. He contained the lab that mixed the shades and placed them in humanity for His liking. Only the foolish man questions God regarding His choices and decisions. It His world! We are just privileged to live in it. We don't get a vote or a right to judge or complain about any people made of God. He delights in the choices of people He made. If we want to come correct with God rather than out of alignment with His will and purpose for our individual and collective lives as race; we'd better get with Him on His side of the fence regarding the race and color of a human life. The shades of man are a variety and a delight to God. He will accept no other opinion from us!

HATE

A man sinks to no deeper lows when he reduces himself to hate. This is the complete opposite end of why God created him. He's misused the purpose of his life. He is vastly out of the will of God.

Regardless of who he hates and why he hates; he's wrong! There's never a reason that will justify his hate. Somewhere along the line, hatred was taught or welcomed in his life through un-for-giveness, ignorance or unawareness.

No matter who he is, not matter why, what or the reason; his hatred is a stench in the nostrils of God. Whether that hate be for crimes of a generation past, of a people, or an incident of today...A man is wrong in his hatred.

Such a man will one day kneel before a Holy God and be asked why he hated. No reason, no excuse, no justification will be allowed by God. No excuse! He'll say, "There was never any justification for your hatred! Your hatred was a product of your feelings which were grossly misaligned." God will inform such a man of all the times He sent others to teach him and to show him that only love was the way. But he ignored the message and the messenger.

But it will be too late when such a man crosses the barrier from life to death. Then he will kneel before God, who holds the power of his eternal destiny, both helpless and hopeless. His hate will be his ticket to eternity.

This could be such a message sent by God as a warning to get it right before that day. All feelings aside, this is not a decision which can be left to our feelings. Unfortunately, most of us wrongly live our lives based on our feelings rather than truth. This decision must be made from truth.

Whether learned, taught, borrowed or welcome...Hatred of no man will be tolerated in the site of God, the Maker of All Men!

HATRED IS LEARNED...NOT INHERITED

A child is born innocent. It knows nothing but of hunger and discomfort. It knows nothing of race or nationality. Neither does it know the color of its own skin. A child comes into this world empty and innocent. We as its parents fill it with good or evil.

A child knows nothing of hatred. It doesn't come into this world hating. It has a mind that must be taught and influenced. The nature of the child is to love and to be loved. This nature must be bent to teach a child hatred. It goes against everything the child was meant to be. All of its receptors are designed and built to love. Someone must go far out of their way to modify and damage the makeup of a child to teach them to hate.

Hatred is learned, not inherited! At the developmental stages of its life, a child mimics what it see's from its parents. The saddest part of this is a child may grow up seeing prejudice and hatred from within its family and believe it's natural to hate people that are different and unlike its own color. This may be all the child knows because it's all they've seen and heard. The sad truth is...They may grow up not even knowing why they hate!

The child may not have known that it had a choice not to hate. But it's what it's environment preached and drilled into them. By the time they're adults, they're full of hate and prejudice and not even knowing the reason why. Other than just because, and it's what they were told.

Hatred stems from ignorance and refusing to understand a person or a people. It's neglect at its farthest end. It's refusing to make an effort to know different. It's rebellion in the sight of God. It's a slap in the face of God. It's rebellion towards what He created. It's wrong on all levels!

A man must one day decide for himself. He must open his eyes to truth. That truth is that God objects to hatred of any people on any level. It doesn't even matter what the people or person's done to warrant the hatred. Hatred will never be justified by any of us in the sight of God.

A man stoops to new levels when he hates. A man raises himself above others when he believes he or the race he represents is better or superior to another. Humanity is the superior race! Individuals with love, compassion, understanding, care and concern for all people are superior beings. Not a particular race; but individuals with hearts of love for all of mankind.

Today our youth have grasped this concept more than any other generation. They don't see color...They only see people! Today families are blended like never before. Some who hated in the past have now found themselves grandparents and great grandparents of children mixed with black and white parents.

A child's been used to destroy the barrier of prejudice and hatred. It's like the wars fought in times of old. A compromise was made by the marriage of children on both sides of the battle. The marriage now served as a bridge to keep the two families from killing each other because their families were now united. It was a wise thing to do.

Somehow our youth have adopted this same philosophy whether or not by their choice, but by their love. They've blended our races and the children produced within the bond have bridged our families and our races. The child dispelled the ignorance through its love and being. It served as an offering of love to rid us of our prejudices and hatred. It's hard to look into the eyes of a child knowing that your blood runs through it and still find hatred in your heart. It's just not possible!

If it is, such a person has gone to some dark places in their heart which only God can bring them back from. The rest of us will not waste our lives with prejudice and hatred and will welcome the gift of love through any and all people.

Chapter 10

We Must Know

~~

Feelings...have the least to do with love! Yet they're the one thing we base love upon the most!

IF WE SAY WE LOVE

I wonder if we really know what it means to love? Sometimes we use this word so casually that our actions don't correspond to the word. Do we know the true meaning of what love really is? Have we been shown the right examples?

To know and truly understand love, we must go to the Source of all love...God. It would seem that the only appropriate way to measure love is to use God's standard. This standard may be different than we think. It may be different than we've been shown. We may have a totally different perception of what it truly means to love. I know I did until God showed me otherwise.

God gave me a formula for love. This is the measuring device to use if we say we love someone. The formula He gave me is $L=ae-s\sim$. Or in simpler terms, Love = Actions X Effort -Selfishness Continuously. This is the formula God uses with us and the example of this is the cross.

He loves us. He took action by sending His own sinless Son to die for the sins of humanity. His efforts reached across nationalities, genders and people. His selfless act to become the perfect sacrificial lamb required by God for the redemption of man, putting us back in the original place of Adam with fellowship with God, was without a doubt the most unselfish deed ever done by any man. He forsook His will to do the will of His father God, for us. He that knew no sin became the sin debt for humanity.

Maybe we'll use this word appropriately now that we understand it's true meaning. Now, if we say we love someone, we have the stick in which to measure it with...The Cross! We now have the formula that God gave us through the cross, L=ae-s~.

Say you love someone? This is the criteria. These are the requirements; especially in marriage. Use this formula before standing before God and saying "I do." These are the standards of love required by husband and wife until only deaths separates them. It's a standard which requires continuous work and unselfishness.

It's not for the weak and selfish, and those that believe that a relationship will sustain itself without continuous effort. It's not for those who aren't prepared to endure the storms of life together and come out stronger as one. It's not for those who are ill prepared to lay down their agenda's for the agenda God has for the couple, not the one. It's not for those that can't see themselves married to this same person for life.

These are the hard questions we must ask ourselves before we possibly damage the life of another living soul. This formula is the standard of love God requires in all of our relationships. In each of them, we must ask ourselves, are we meeting the requirements of love? If not, now we know what it takes on our part. Once we know, we're held accountable.

I'VE BEEN MISLED

They misled me! They've taken me to distant and unfamiliar roads. They were excellent leaders, but very poor followers. They were...My Feelings!

They've been the builder of the emotional roller coaster in my life. Up and down, sideways, twist and turns. They've been the cause of unwelcome guest such as bitterness, resentment and unforgiveness in my life.

Being led by them, I've lived my life inside out. They've been the cause of my immaturity, bad decisions and poor judgment. They've brought something terrible with them called Pride. Pride made me hold on to things when I should have let go. They've caused me to keep my silence when I should have spoken and said "I'm sorry!"

God never intended for me to live by my feelings. He never intended for me to base my relationships completely on them either. Feelings are very strong and very powerful emotions, but they're very poor decision makers. Feelings are products of my flesh. I was never intended to live by my flesh. It will only steer me in wrong directions and the opposite direction of God.

If I base my decisions on my feelings, my decisions will be skewed and misaligned. Feelings can be all over the grid of emotions. Emotions can cause me to make decisions I'll only regret later. They may not be in the best interest of me or the other person involved.

Wisdom and knowledge are the best foundations in which to make decisions. This takes my feelings from subjective to factual. (Subjective meaning, based on how I feel or what I believe to be right.) (Factual meaning, based on truthful information supported by evidence.)

I'm thankful for my feelings and emotions because they remind me I'm alive and living. But even feelings and emotions have their place in life. For too long, they've been the basis of many of my decisions, whether right or wrong. But I'm not trying to live like that anymore. I've hurt others in the process and made a mess out of things in my own life.

Feelings must release the reins of leadership in my life and take their proper place as followers. It's then I live my life right side out and base my decisions on seeking God's wisdom and not the poor leaders of my flesh.

ATTITUDE

It can be the worst part of me. Sometimes you see it first before you ever get close to me. It has run more people away than ever wanted to make them stay...It's my attitude!

A nice one is pleasant, but a nasty one; who can bear! It's been the greatest cause of people not wanting to be around us and even avoiding us. We weren't born like this of course, but through hurts and time, we've become full of it. It's our attitudes. It's what we display to others and the world. It shows through our dispositions and personalities. Many are the result of walls we build in our lives to prevent others from hurting us. They end up doing more damage in our lives than good.

None of us want to get hurt. It's something we all would avoid if we could. But life is cruel sometimes. It comes with both pains and disappointments. People can be cruel in life. Not all are good to us. Not all are good for us. Unfortunately, some people come with their own agendas in our lives. They want something from us. They'll even lie and deceive us to get it.

Some people are pretty good liars! Today we call it "Game!" Call it what we want, God calls it foolishness, manipulation and lies! When we fall for it, the results can be devastating. Falls lead to injuries, hurt and pain. The pain others cause us that we don't deal with and forgive, can lead to being a wall around our hearts.

Our hearts were never designed to be prisoners behind walls. God designed the ribs of bone to protect our physical hearts. He would design wisdom, knowledge and discernment to protect our emotional hearts.

Our hearts are where we live and breathe! They weren't meant to be hidden behind barriers. Our hearts were made to be free, exposed and vulnerable, just like God's. His heart is never covered, but always exposed, even though we constantly hurt Him through rejection and disobedience. Yet, His arms and heart are always wide open to receive us with love and compassion. The Heart of God has a door on it that never closes.

Today's society is so messed up that we're taught that exposing our hearts to love and concern is a sign of weakness. Especially when we as men do it! That's a complete lie! Would we tell God and Jesus that they're weak? Their hearts are exposed constantly with care and concern for humanity!

We've got to stop believing the lies of the world. These lies will only keep us living beneath our privileges as sons and daughters of

God. They will keep us in the bondage of fear and cause us to hide our hearts rather than display them freely.

Where we mess up is through ignorance. Our hearts aren't for everyone, but just for One. If we don't take the time to seek God's direction for the one, we'll end up back in our rooms building walls around our hearts which will show through our hearts and personalities. Otherwise known as...Attitudes!

NO LOVE WITHOUT EXPOSURE

We live in a world where right is wrong and wrong is right. It's a backwards world where truth gets ushered out the door for convenience.

The ways of God are foolish to the world and always have been. It's why He tells us we're to be a "Peculiar People!" We're not meant to go along with the practices of the world. We're not meant to fit in. We're meant to stand out!

Standing out doesn't mean we're fanatics, loud and forcing God onto others. How can we do that to others when God Himself doesn't do it to us! He merely presents Himself to us and gives us the choice to accept Him or not. How does God present this choice to us? In what manner does He display it to us? He does it through one word...Vulnerability!

Contrary to our beliefs, love is not a feeling! Love is a demonstration of acts; not a word. Feelings are a residual of love; not love itself! The greatest display of love is the outstretched arms of a Holy God to a sinful people. We say we love, but do we really know what that means?

To see a true display of love we can't look amongst ourselves to find it. We must only look to God as our Source and example of what love really is. Love is the exposure of our hearts whether that love is reciprocated or not. Love needs no motive. Love in return is not a prerequisite of love. Love is...Regardless!

Love is the vulnerability of our hearts and souls. It's when we show ourselves in our true essence without pride or reservation. There's no love without vulnerability and exposure. These are the demonstrative deeds which display love. Without them, love is just a word; a noun rather than a verb.

Our love can't be a noun. I learned in elementary school that a noun is a person, place or thing. I also learned in that same school that a verb requires action. A verb is an action word, my teacher use to say. No matter how we slice it, there's no love without the demonstration of acts which follow and are in alignment with our words.

Contrary to the views of the world, love is the strongest deed on earth. There's nothing weak about it. It's not something for the weak. Love is for the strong! Love is for those willing to display their hearts at great risk. That alone requires tremendous strength.

Our hearts are the most delicate instruments in our bodies. When our heart stops beating, we cease to live. While we live, our hearts are alive and ready to display and receive love. What have we gained if we love only those that love us? This is not the measure of love. Love knows no bounds. It has no limits.

To be loved in return is neither a requirement nor a condition of love. God loves us in spite of our rebellion and disobedience towards Him. It was Him that we sinned against and disobeyed all of our lives, until we found Him through Christ.

It was Him, with His heart fully exposed; vulnerable to humanity...Loving us regardless of ourselves!

This is the measure of true Love...Vulnerability and Exposure!

THE MOST UNATTRACTIVE PERSON I'VE EVER SEEN

This man had the nerve to be arrogant. He thought he was All That! He thought he looked good. He tried to hide his unattractiveness by dressing sharp, riding around in nice cars or having the finer things in life.

Sometimes he even tried to mask his unattractiveness by having a beautiful woman on his arm.

It was hideous to look upon him. I hate to talk about people, but he was disgusting looking!

Did I see this man in the circus? No...I saw him in the mirror! The last thing any of us truly want to see...Is Ourselves!

THE TIME WE'RE ABSENT

The time we're absent in a young child's life seems to double if not triple, as they're advancing faster than any other time in their lives. Days to us could seem like weeks to them. These are critical bonding times in a child's young life!

We can be there and cement the bond for life...Or be absent and lose it!

HAVE TO BE'S

It's a prayer of convenience. God's not even in the equation. We don't want to move, act, sacrifice or do anything to receive our mate. We just want God to drop him or her into our laps and on our doorsteps.

It's unrealistic! Then we wonder why we end up with such messes in our lives. We look at God in disgust and disappointment and wonder why our relationships constantly fail. God wasn't consulted! He wasn't allowed in the equation. We simply gave Him a list of our prerequisites and requirements as if He were Santa Claus or a Genie.

Off we go thinking that we've done something great and fulfilled our obligations of asking God for a mate, by laying a laundry list of "Have To Be's" at His feet.

God looks at this list, and even His hands are tied from blessing us. In our selfish ways and schemes of wanting our perfect mate, there's one thing we overlook...God won't bless us with mess! God don't bless with mess. We get into the mess when we charge ahead like a bull in a china shop with our "Have To Be's!" We make this choice, not God.

We tied His hands when we sent Him that unrealistic and selfish Christmas list. We've locked Him out of the decision making process, because there's one line that even God won't cross with us as human's...Our free will to choose and make decisions on our own.

There's a solution to all of this. There's a way to make things right and get in alignment with God's will for our lives and marriages. The answer is humility! The answer is surrendering our will

127

to God instead of giving a him a huge list of requirements. Instead, we must trust Him in knowing what we want before we even ask Him. The Bible tells us He knows our thoughts and even the desires of our hearts before we ask Him. So faith has to be a part of this equation.

There's nothing lazy about faith, as we may have previously believed. Now that we've asked for God's guidance, help and direction; now that we've given Him His job of decision making back, we still have a part to play in this. So many of us misinterpret the scripture when it tells us to "Be still and wait on God." Being still means to cease to maneuver in our own strength, ways and decision making. It doesn't mean to take a vacation while God does all the work.

We perish for the lack of understanding of God's word. We miss out due to ignorance and misinterpretation. We'll always have an active part in everything God is doing in our lives, for our purpose and towards our destiny. God can do whatever He wants; but for the most part, we have work to do in the blessings He sends us.

If we're asking God for our mate, then we have to do our part and not expect God to just drop him or her out of the sky, or to receive an "Adamic" operation while we're put to sleep and God takes one of our ribs and we awaken to the arms of our spouses. That's not going to happen! God always expects us to work with His plans and purposes for our lives and not just sit and wait.

While we wait, we must prepare for our mates. The first thing we must do is allow God to clean house within us. Most of us have a lot of junk and baggage within us from past hurts and bad relationships. If these hurts aren't addressed and forgiven, they leave the scars of bitterness and resentment. They can also leave insecurities within us that we can wrongly place on our mate when anything they do reminds us of the pain others did to us. It's not fair to take old hurts into a new relationship, just as the Bible tells us the story of putting new wine in old bottles.

We must be prepared for new. This mate that God sends us will be a new relationship. It will be a relationship closer than any on earth. Why would we bring old junk into it, just to ruin it? We need to be healed first! First we need to be fixed, repaired and prepared.

If not, we're heading down another destructive and devastating road called Divorce!

We've got to move from our selfish ways and desires. Marriage works only if God begins and remains in the equation. We must remain out of it; meaning our flesh. Marriage is not, and can't be reduced to a flesh decision. It's a spiritual union and must be a spiritual decision. The magnitude and importance of this decision must be left in the hands of God...Not our own!

We must kneel before God and humbly ask Him to prepare us for our mate. We must confess all un-forgiveness of past loves and relationships. We must let go of any anger, hatred or bitterness we carry for anyone that's hurt us in the past or present. We must clear out our hearts and make room to receive love and prepare to give it without limit nor regret.

We must get out of the business of telling God, instead of activity seeking His will for our lives and our spouses. Telling God to give us what we want is arrogance on our part. We're talking to an Omniscient God, who knows and see's all. What could we ever tell Him that He doesn't already know? We must humble ourselves before a Holy God. We must come to the place of letting go and trust with God. We must know that His ways are better than ours. We must know who and what He has for us will be better than we could have chosen for ourselves.

No more of this, "God I'm not moving, my mate better be within 50 miles of me!" "She's gotta know her place in this marriage and do what I want her to do!" "We're getting married, but I'm keeping my last name!" "I'll just change him after we're married!" "Unless he's 6'4", he might as well keep steppin. I may only be 4'5", but I want a tall man on my side!" Imagine being God and hearing this foolishness! I've been on a dating site before and these are things I've seen for myself and heard them in disgust from disappointed women.

A small minority say "I'm willing to submit my life to God through this man in marriage and I'm willing to relocate if this is the will of God." "I want to love this woman as Christ loved the church and am willing to meet her needs before my own!" Very few have reached this point. Yet, it's the place we all need to be if we plan on being married and blessed by God in marriage.

These are the ones that get it! These are the ones that have laid their will at the feet of God where they belong. These are the ones that have taken both self and selfishness out of the equation and given God the liberty and freedom to bless them with the best thing that's ever happened to them! No list of "Have To Be's," but a humble spirit before the Lord, wanting His will and His desire to bless them.

Chapter 11

Unity

~

It's been the weapon of choice for centuries. It has killed more than any weapon ever created. It is the weapon of Mass Destruction...It is Hate!

WHEN WE STAND

When we stand confident, proud Sons and Daughters of God knowing who we are, knowing our purpose to bring forth good in life and the world...

When we stand confident with humility, and not with arrogance, as a people knowing and understanding that it was the plan of God to bring us here to be a part of and to significantly contribute to this land...

When we are assured of our combined heritage from Africa and our heritage here as Americans, and live in peace and forgiveness with the wrongs done to our people...

We are now Americans who originated from Africa through the horrible bonds of slavery. Nevertheless, this is the home God has chosen for us.

Then, we can stand and join the other races that occupy and maintain this great land as United Citizen of these United States...

Standing arm in arm, shoulder to shoulder, hand in hand, joined for the cause of preserving this land, life, and the lifestyles all of our ancestors lived for, fought for and died for.

OUR MORAL CENTER

There are good people in all races. There's bad in all. We will mature as humanity when we base our likes and dislikes on an individual basis rather than the basis of race. Let a man's, a woman's character be the basis on which they stand; but never on the pigmentation of their skin.

It's the heart of a man that either makes him good or evil...Not his skin color. The color of his skin has no decision making capabilities. Those issues come forth from the brain through the recesses of the heart. Any racial hatred or indifference is a heart issue. It stems from a bad heart, not from its valves and chambers...But it's moral center!

When we stand for Only the rights and privileges of our own race... We're just as wrong as those that hate!

LEST WE FORGET

There's one very important fact that we must always remember when the dust of injustice was wiped away from our people. Not that all of it has cleared, but at least we can now see ourselves, know where we've come from and know where we need to go. The one thing we must remember and acknowledge is...Our White Brothers and Sisters!

Let's dispel this myth right now, this lie, this untruth...That all whites were evil and all blacks were good. There's good and evil in all of us. Evil isn't prejudice, and doesn't distinguish who it uses based on color. Evil hates without a cause or a reason. It's just what it does.

Let it be known from this day forward, that if it weren't for our white brothers and sisters who hated slavery, who hated injustice done to any race, who stood with us when we stood...We wouldn't have what we have today!

As good as we were as a people, as intelligent, and as much as we had to offer, it was only untapped potential if someone didn't stand up and give us a chance. After all, it was their land, their jobs, their money and all they owned, that we needed to survive when the law set our people free. Whites were far more generous than we ever acknowledge them to be. We only look back and remember those filled with prejudice and hatred. Who we forget about are those that helped us along the way.

Not all slave owners were evil. Not all treated their slaves like property. Some were victims of the times in which they lived. Could they afford to hire workers when everyone else was getting their labor for free? Maybe some had to purchase slaves just to compete in business. Maybe they hated it. Maybe they had no financial choice but to have slaves. Maybe these were the ones that treated their slaves as people instead of property. Maybe these were the ones that died and set their slaves free in their wills and even left them property and land for them to start life on their own.

It's wrong for us to believe that all whites were evil just as it's wrong to believe that all blacks were good. It's just not true!

To come together as a people of these United States without regard to race or color, we must first reach back before we can step forward. We must reach back in time and remove this stereotype from the white race as they must remove the ones from ours. Stereotypes are lies. Only proven facts are true.

Our white brothers and sisters are full of love and we have so many of them to thank for not going along with the evil and injustices in the times of our ancestors. They saw us as people and children of God. They gave us chances and opportunities. They significantly contributed to our status in life today. Just as there are things that we would like to forget, there are facts that we must also remember.

We have our places today due to the good in those not of our own color. We couldn't lift ourselves out of slavery. We needed a hand. That was a White hand clinched within ours. God always has His people looking out for the injustice of any people.

We must first heal in order to Unite! Healing is the prerequisite to being united. We must allow truth, not stereotypes to propel us forward. We must see the entire picture, not only pieces of it. We must no longer be blind to those that helped us rise, who helped us achieve and advance. They were there, all along our paths with us, with hands and opportunities.

Time has come for the truth. Time has come to welcome, acknowledge, to thank and embrace our white sisters and brothers, because they too have been treated unfairly. I'm not talking about the ones full of hate and those that did horrible acts to our people. Even those, we still must forgive! This didn't make up an entire race of people.

There were countless innocent ones that we've just lumped in with everyone else. That's just as wrong on our part. All haven't wronged us! We've not been good to all! We're not here to tally up wrongs, neither to compare them. Hate is wrong in any capacity whether we believe we're justified to hate or not. God says it's wrong, and we'll answer to Him if hate is found within us.

If we reduce ourselves to dislike a man, let it be for his character and his heart; but never for his skin color. His color is a non factor in the matter. It's his heart that's the culprit!

Let's stop throwing the blanket of hating and disliking over entire races of people for their color or the past deeds of their ancestors. Let maturity be found in each of us as individuals and let a man stand or fail based on his own merit, and not the race he represents.

God gave Dr. King a Dream...He gave me a Vision!

A NATIONAL UNITY DAY

Our country is over 200 years old. We are the United States of America and we have never celebrated our Unity; Our Independence, yes, but never our unity; our ability to be many, yet one, from various backgrounds, nationalities and races.

Let's celebrate our differences as people and not isolate ourselves because of them. Let's celebrate Unity Day as a nation! Let's do this in the name of the 11 Black Soldiers known as the Wereth 11, who were tortured, mutilated and murdered in WWII; the Battle of the Bulge. Out of the tremendous hatred done to these 11 soldiers; let's honor their sacrifices and their memories in Peace, in Unity and in Forgiveness.

Let their deaths be remembered as a symbol of unity for us all. Let their lives stand for something, to push us towards peace and togetherness. There's been enough hate in the world to where another act...Would be too many!

I propose that one day there would be a National Unity Day. From the state of West Virginia, that gave us Anna Jarvis, the founder of Mother's Day and Nancy Hanks, the mother of the man who penned The Emancipation Proclamation, our 16th President, Abraham Lincoln, let UNITY DAY start here and spread throughout all states in this great Nation.

Let's leave this world in a better place for our children and our grandchildren coming behind us. Let's think of their lives and their world too.

Let's all celebrate our membership of just One Race...The Human Race!

UNITY & FORGIVENESS

Unity starts with forgiveness. There have been wrong in all races, from all sides. We mustn't tally up the wrongs of the past. We must not forget them either. What we must do is remember them out of wisdom, so they're never repeated.

Some of us are still harboring bitterness over what was done to our ancestors hundreds of years ago. Yes, those things were wrong! They were cruel and inhumane. But they were their mistakes...Not Ours! We have a choice today whether to keep looking back or to start moving forward. We can't change the past! That's out of our control. What we can do is change the future. We can make a difference right now by letting go. We can choose to let go of the pains of our past. It's simply a choice we must make by an act of our will.

Bitterness never profits anyone. It's a cancer that slowly eats away at our hearts, at our emotions, with our ability to care and with life itself. It erodes life rather than building it. It's bondage rather than freedom.

Our ancestors had their day to make the world a better place. Some of them took the right paths, many of them didn't. They lived their lives. Let's not let them continue to live ours.

Most people hate and don't even know why they hate. Many hate because they were taught wrongly to hate. So they grew up hating because it was instilled within them, rather than being given the choice to know that hate is wrong.

This is our day! This is our time to decide for ourselves to make this world better for our descendants coming behind us. Today we can make the choice to Unify rather than Divide. We create our world! Not those who made the mistakes long ago.

Let's remember their wrongs and even teach them, but let's be a better generation for Unity. It's time we start making choices for ourselves instead of living in the past. Let's say goodbye to both bigotry and bitterness. Let's leave them where they belong...In The Past!

Our tomorrow starts today!

LET US BE THE ONES

Our forefathers started something that's continued throughout the generations. It's called Racism! It's seeing another race of people less, inferior or unwelcomed. It was wrong! Not all of our ancestors were good, nor had good intentions. Some had hearts which were evil and encouraged and convinced others to buy into their evil ways and ideals.

That was their generation. This is ours! We can be the generation that reverses these evil trends. It's foolish for us to continue something we know is wrong simply because people who lived before us did it. Because they did it, because they started it, doesn't make it right. It was never, nor will be right in the eyes of God.

There are many reasons for hate. None of them are justified to God. Our differences are one of the main factors which initiated hatred. It was our forefather's inability or unwillingness to take the time and make the effort to embrace the differences of another human being. Instead, they deemed themselves superior and those different inferior. The majority rules, whether right or wrong. The strongest dominates and forces their will upon the weak.

In our communities, we have many races from various backgrounds. We as the majority shouldn't see the less in number as different...But as Neighbors! We have the opportunity today to put the foolishness of race and differences behind us. We're the generations that can make a difference!

Yes, we've had many ancestors to do some tremendous things. We've also had many which perpetuated evil born in their own hearts and forced it upon the few, the weak and the less fortunate. We must open our eyes to the good and the bad of our history, to continue the good and stop the evil. Just because someone from our past did something doesn't make it right. It doesn't mean those acts should continue.

Let's be the generations to fix this. Let's be the people to employ embracing rather than dividing. Difference is the Hand of God upon humanity. Let's be remembered by the generations behind us as the generations that took a stand, that got it right, that fixed what our forefathers ruined.

Let's be the generation that fulfills the words of The Constitution..."That All Men Are Created Equal!" Let's be the ones to veer off the path of wrongs and take us on the new road to Unity & Peace!

PREAMBLE TO MEMORANDUM OF UNDERSTANDING

May this serve as an apology from the living descendants of those who violently stood against the Black race when we dared to stand up for our civil rights. When we dared to take a stand for rights granted to us a century early, but was never put into action.

May this serve as an apology once and for all from those who released fire hoses and dogs on the Black race. May this serve as an apology for the lynching and raping of our people. May it serve as an apology for the deaths, death threats and brutality that our people endured not so many years ago.

This has caused bitterness, resentment and hatred within our people that we're required to forgive with or without a formal apology; in order that we may move forward to maturity, growth and character development. We are required by God to forgive the atrocious acts done upon our people both during Slavery and the Civil Rights Movement. We must forgive and move forward!

Even if an apology comes formally or not, we as the Black race are required to forgive within our own hearts and move forward. This requirement of moving forward without acknowledgement or the requirement of an apology is the requirement of God, not man. Man will have us to continue to hold onto the bitterness and to keep the tension brewing. God will not!

This is God's requirement for us to finally be set free by Pharaoh and moving our lives figuratively out of our Egypt. Don't die in bondage in Egypt another day expecting an acknowledgement or an apology. Make the choice to forgive the wrong, move forward, release the bitterness, hatred and tension, and find yourself a new person without a life of resentment. Let your new life now be found in Peace, Maturity and Freedom!

In order for there to be peace in these United States, there must be acknowledgement of these vicious acts upon the Black race. What was done to the Native Americans is a totally different act of injustice that I pray God will allow me to address at a later time.

Let's acknowledge that we're not natives, but citizens of this land. We must acknowledge that this is the home chosen for us by God and that it's His requirement that we live here together as Equal and Valuable citizens. We must also acknowledge that it's the will of man, not God to go against this plan by the degradation and with-holding of the rights of any people regardless of their origin, color or gender.

Let this document serve as The Document that will finally unite us as one people of these United States. May it finally fulfill the documents penned by our founding forefathers with or without the intent to exclude a situation or a people as Equal and Valuable citizens of this land.

Finally, let's put these unspoken, un-addressed and unacknowledged issues of race behind us. Let's place them on the table of acknowledgement, recognition and maturity so they no longer serve as ghosts of our past that we refuse to recognize. Until they are addressed and acknowledged by us, they'll continue to appear to us as the cries of the dead who were treated unjustly and unfair in cruel and unimaginable ways.

We must be the generation to finally silence their cries. We must be the ones to finally give them their rest and honor in death by correcting the wrongs of their generation and making things right in ours. It's time! This has been swept under the carpet for too long. Today is our day to correct our past by changing our future with no more racial tension, but racial peace.

MEMORANDUM OF UNDERSTANDING

To all who may see these words...Greetings! Let this document serve as a Memorandum of Understanding specifically between the white and black races who settled, survived and lived within the continent of North America from its inception to its eternity. Although untimely, late and extremely tardy, let it come into effect immediately to govern the relations, the living arrangements and the sharing of this great continent of North America of All People!

Let it first be said and recognized that God, not man is the creator of all men. Being a God of love, He would never differentiate between one of His creations or another. He would find them all Equal and Valuable! With this being said, there would never become a place in time where one race of people would be deemed superior over another. It would suffice that there would only be superior individuals, exhibited through the qualities of their character, with the purpose to enhance humanity through love, care and compassion for their fellowman.

In the sight of Almighty God, Supreme and Infinite Father, every man born on this earth would stand equal to every man with no distinction to his color or race, but would only divide and distinguish himself by the deeds he performs for good or evil.

Let this Memorandum of Understanding serve as an apology Once and For All, by the evil men who represented the white race at the time of slavery, for the wrongs, the humiliation, the degradation, the injustice and the harm performed on the Black Africans which were forced against their will and arrived in this land in chains, rather than being welcomed.

May it serve as an apology for every stripe on the backs of slaves. May it serve as an apology for the raping of every black slave woman. Let it serve as an apology for separating and dividing the families of slaves to degrade or to control, or simply for financial gain.

Let this memorandum serve as an apology for robbing the Black African's of their homes, their heritages, their customs and the land in which they were born, to be reduced to the lowest form of humanity as slaves and free labor.

Let this Memorandum of Understanding, Once and For All, serve as The Apology of those with evil hearts representing the White race, and The Acceptance of The Apology from the Descendants of Slaves of the Black race which endured such cruelties and hardships.

With confession and forgiveness, let there now be advancement!

We the people and descendants of wrongs done to a people as slaves, now have the opportunity to advance and to unite our races. We have both opportunity and chance to correct the wrongs of our ancestors; knowing that it is the Will of God for All men to live together peacefully. Knowing that God doesn't see color, He only sees the heart of the individual. Knowing that the shades we display on the exterior of our bodies is the handiwork of God's creativity, not to be used as a tool of exclusion and prejudice by man.

We must know and understand that it was the plan of God, not the hearts of evil man, to bring the black race to this land for the benefit and enhancement of this nation. It was the plan of God, that people of All races who believed in unity could come to this land and be accepted.

Furthermore, let it be established that this land was founded upon the principals of serving and worshipping God Almighty in freedom without conviction.

May we as all people of these United States resign to the fact that the Maker of Heaven, Earth and Mankind, ordained that we both, white and black races live here together on this continent with acceptance and no longer just tolerance. May we embrace our differences as gifts of distinction for the betterment of humanity. May we no longer void the letter and the intent of the Constitution designed to form the character of each individual in this nation, to uphold its obligation to consider every man of God's creation Equal and Valuable contributors of both life and society, regardless of his race, color, creed, religious preference or gender. May we be the generation which fulfills the words and the letters of The Constitution by abolishing prejudice, hatred and injustice to any race of people.

Although we weren't the ones who penned it...Let us be the ones to fulfill its obligations, promises and decrees!

Let us rise as better people. Let us stand for every man and not just our own. Let us put aside our differences and break the bread of common fellowship with peace and love. Let's tear down the walls that have stood so strong between us. Let us with hammer, chisel and device; destroy these barriers of separation, misunderstandings and misconceptions.

May we with wisdom find that the breath of Adam breathes in all of us eternally; that we all originated from one Source, one man, one Father. Let color no longer be the barrier between us. Let it serve simply as the variety of choice by God. Let's see the difference of race with the purpose of God; only to take us a further distant from our father Adam so we could populate the earth without being too close to our kin.

Let all who read this, or come in proximity of these words, know this day is a new day. Let all know that these words symbolize a new beginning. However late, let them serve as a bridge for humanity, and justice for all living souls without distinction or prejudice.

Once and for all, for mankind, may these words serve as an apology of a White race long gone; a people who carried out the evil deeds within their own hearts, motivated by greed and selfishness. Let this be a confession of wrong and accountability to those living of the Black race for the cruelties performed upon our people.

Once and for all, for mankind, may these words be accepted as an apology for a Black people long gone; a people who endured the evil thrust upon them in unimaginable ways. Let this be an acknowledgement of those wrongs and an acceptance of an apology from the descendants of the perpetrators. Let these words serve as a gesture of responsibility to relieve us, as representatives of the black race, of any bitterness, anger, contempt, aggression, and let it now bring forth forgiveness and peace.

May we as people of God, rather than people of race, no longer seek to serve a personal or racial agenda, but let our thoughts and actions include all living beings in our current and future plans. May we put aside anything that would seek to divide us. May we obey the decree of God to live together in peace and good will towards all men.

Let this day be the day that the barrier of color no longer divides us, but unites us as a variety of people blended by the Hand of God Himself!

Chapter 12

At Your Feet Lord

Many of us stand before God when our rightful places are only...At His Feet!

THE MINISTER'S PRAYER

I will minister to you in humility. I have not arrived! The only position I seek is to remain at the feet of Jesus. I don't seek a stage or an audience...I'm not an entertainer.

I would rather prepare you than impress you. I would rather provoke deliverance than applause. It's my prayer that you find meaning in my message, not the delivery of it.

I will not confuse the blessings of God with numbers and finance. Great oratory skills would give me the ability to preach, but not always to minister. I would rather minister than preach that lives would be changed.

Stirring deliveries excite but do they change us? My attempts must not be to please the congregation, but to please God. If my goal is only to stir and excite...Then I've missed the mark! What purpose does it serve if we exits the church no different than we entered?

I stand as one of you. I'm not exempt from the message I deliver. The only difference between me and you is that I heard it first. Jesus was the only one entitled to use the word "You" as He ministered.

The rest of us are only authorized to use the words "Us or We" as we minister.

If I stand before you as if I have no fault, then I'm the one in most need of prayer.

My greatest desire is that people would behold God through my ministry in all of His glory and splendor, and I become a spectator in my own body...Never wanting to be seen!

PRECIOUS GIFTS

There was a man who was given two precious gifts from God. When he stood in the line to receive his gifts with the other children of God, others were so proud and boastful about the gifts they received from Him. Some had gifts of ministry, some prophesy; others the gifts of faith and healing.

They all left proudly before God and looked down on the one left standing in line with his two gifts that no one else wanted. He looked in his bag and then looked at God and said, "Do you not love me too Lord?"

But God said, "I have a special gift for you. You've been set apart for a great purpose. The gifts I've given you are greater than any of the gifts the others received. You see, they'll receive their gifts and walk in them and at some point forget where their gifts came from. People will begin to praise them for their gifts and soon they'll believe it's them and not my gifts given to them."

"But you my son are not just called, but chosen. You've been chosen for a task far greater than yourself. The task you've been called for will affect countless lives, not just a few. And when others attempt to praise you, you'll step back with humility and say, oh no, these gifts aren't mine but the Master's."

"Because of the two gifts in your bag, arrogance and pride will never be a problem for you. Unlike the others, they'll constantly wrestle between humility and arrogance. You see son, they just wanted the gifts, you wanted Me and much more. They got what they wanted but can never fully walk in their gifts because they didn't take the time to receive the two gifts you have in your bag."

"No man's gifts can work effectively without these two special gifts, yet they're something no man wants."

The young man opened his bag and in it were two small gifts. The gifts were full of dust from sitting on the shelf, because they were the least popular of all God's gifts. The humble servant reached into his bag and gladly embraced his two priceless gifts from God.

They were the gifts of Brokenness and Humility!

BEING GREAT

In these times we have confused greatness with fame and the ability to entertain, which have little to nothing to do with the word. We so easily bestow upon those undeserving, and ignore those who truly warrant. The greatest men are not the richest, most powerful or most famous...But he who finds the least within himself to bow down and serve others.

No man has ever served in any greater role or position than that of a Servant. Greatness is never found in he that serves himself.

Jesus was a sinless, perfect man, yet He deflected the title of being "Good" others tried to bestow upon Him and indicated that there was only One worthy of that title, that was God Himself. This lets us all know where we stand.

We're merely stewards over good works God placed within us. Those of us that would seek to be the greatest should seek to be the least in the eyes of God. At the feet of Jesus, is the highest place obtainable.

THE HIGHEST PRAISE

When I kneel in prayer to God, He often speaks to me and I get up and assume my duties as His scribe.

As I was telling God how wonderful and amazing He is, He showed me something that I needed to be reminded of. It's the highest praise. The highest praise from me to God will never be through words I utter through my mouth. The highest form of praise I can ever give to God is not through my words, but through my life.

Words are empty unless action is placed behind them. Its only then they become works. My words are empty to God unless my life is an example and a reflection of the words I speak to Him. God is not interested in all the noise I make. He's interested in the results of my life which come to Him as a sweet aroma or a stench in His nostrils.

A sweet aroma comes before God as my life is barren of all arrogance and pride. It's a life of humility before the Lord as His servant desiring to do His work without ever wanting to be seen for it. It's a life of living and knowing that you wouldn't dare accept an ounce of God's praise nor His glory. Your only desire is to please Him and step aside that others may see Him and never yourself.

So let the world shout, scream and holler to God. From spending time with the Master and hearing His voice, I'll take the more silent road of praising God with the deeds of my life rather than numerous words. He is able to sift the many words that I offer to Him in praise and determine if they are wood, hay or stubble anyways.

The God of all creation is not as much interested in our words as He is in the results that our lives that reflect these words. God, my prayer to you is that my life would be found pleasing in your sight as a man with humility that desires for you to receive the glory for the amazing things you do through my life. As your servant, I offer every act of my life that receives the attention and gratitude from others as praise back to you.

May I step aside as the attention of Your works through my life bring attention and recognition to you. For it's You, not I, that is truly deserving and the only one worthy of receiving praise for anything good that will ever transform from my life.

May my life, not idle words be the highest form of praise I could ever give to You.

CPSIA information can be obtained at www.ICGtesting.com
Printed in the USA
BVOW040255310112

281783BV00001B/10/P